Syria

Syrian Women Refugees

*Personal Accounts
of Transition*

OZLEM EZER

McFarland & Company, Inc., Publishers
Jefferson, North Carolina

ISBN (print) 978-1-4766-7585-5
ISBN (ebook) 978-1-4766-3490-6

LIBRARY OF CONGRESS AND BRITISH LIBRARY CATALOGUING DATA ARE AVAILABLE

Front cover illustration by Yara Said

Printed in the United States of America

McFarland & Company, Inc., Publishers
Box 611, Jefferson, North Carolina 28640
www.mcfarlandpub.com

To all displaced, unique, and brave souls
whose bodies are restrained through
borders, paper shuffling, and fingerprinting.

Table of Contents

Acknowledgments

Moving to the U.S. five months after I began my interviews did not seem like the ideal step, but it turned out to be more fruitful than I had imagined. To begin with, I arrived only one week before the coup attempt in July 2016. Leaving Turkey would have been impossible if I had stayed for teaching during the summer. When my application to the UC Center for Middle Eastern Studies proved to be successful, I was able to gather the motivation to continue with the incomplete interviews and added the new ones to the portfolio despite what was going on in Turkey. It wasn't easy. Thanks to the wise and wide ranges of technology use, the Syrian participants shared many hours and pages of biographical information with me regarding their stories. Moreover, my two research assistants, Özge Balkaya and Sevil Şahutoğlu, were available and skillful in their contributions from Turkey.

I will continue to collect and write life stories with the hopes of dismantling stereotypes among people and connecting their narratives to the readers and to each other in ways that nobody is able to foresee, myself included. This is the beauty of writing a book. I feel honored by the trust and the generosity that the co-participants displayed, especially when they looked me in the eye and lowered down their voices, "I'll tell you something, but I don't want it to be in the book." My dear friend, Michelle Morkert, the professor of women's and gender studies at Concordia University Chicago, commented that she'd like to record my life story one day, taking me to the other side of the scale. Her comment kept visiting me whenever a Syrian participant shared intimate moments, tears, and love stories among many other long-buried memories. I have admired their transparency and I was not sure about my ability or courage to do that. Some were hesitant in their responses because they were perfectionists and wanted to perform the best, even when I said there is no "best answer" in a life story interview. Two of them boldly told me to go ahead and use their full names and pictures, which I argued otherwise, but Muzna Dureid insisted.

Two of the potential participants played with the idea of having their stories in print for a while before pulling out. I had one participant in Sweden with an extraordinarily story, but her life was getting too complicated to put into words as the time proceeded. I could feel the pressure of her full-time NGO work in a foreign setting and I respect her choice. For the next volume, I plan to fulfill "the Swedish gap," as I name it, since Sweden's commitment to humanitarian causes needs to be acknowledged more widely.

Özge Balkaya landed in my email like an angel on the day when I figuratively lost the participant from Sweden. *Deus ex machina!* In a long letter, she expressed her strong wish to volunteer for any project as long as I was involved in it despite her demanding job at Sabancı University. Having experienced the aftermath of interviewing traumatized individuals at the Women Peace Makers Program in San Diego back in 2005, I hesitated. In response, Özge agreed to complete a semester-long university course on oral history, read everything I recommended, and regularly sent me her lecture notes and questions. She excelled in her dedication to the cause. I am grateful for the interviews she conducted with Leila in Istanbul.

Sevil Şahutoğlu, another former student, invested a lot of time and labor in two interviews with Zizinia, which took place in the Turkish cities of Gaziantep and Hatay. She proved to be a gentle and practical assistant that every researcher would like to have. She has the gift of connecting to any being on earth and leaving a positive impression, which I hope she will make further use of in the future.

My debt of gratitude extends to the wonderful Berkeley student Joanne Chan for the website assistance (syrianwomanhoods.com) and to the incredible Asma Khalifa (Arabic to English interpreter), who have both been most generous with their time and in answering the dozens of questions with which I showered them. Thank you Diala Halloum for the timely translation of Lutfia's hand-written notes in Arabic and for introducing me to Muzna Dureid. Elizabeth Madsen, Tresa Eyres, Zoe Holman, Mary Ann Whitten, and Anne Gallagher edited the early drafts of several chapters, offering comments and suggestions for which I am deeply grateful. Elizabeth also introduced me to Yara Said, a promising Syrian artist currently based in Amsterdam. Said, initially became known internationally as the designer of the Refugee Olympic Team's flag in 2016, agreed to design the book cover from her sensitive anti–Orientalist perspective. Muzna Dureid shared a few of her own photographs with Said as inspiration, demonstrating her brave stance to go public once again.

Without the financial and spiritual support from Sallie Bingham and Jude Deason, both of whom I met in Santa Fe, this book wouldn't have come to an existence. I hope that one day I can capture my surrogate mothers/fellow-writers/friends' stories in a separate book. My gratitude extends to other angels in disguise who entrusted to me their homes and feline residents. My Muses wither when they are not provided a safe room of their own. Among the members of "My Millennium Medici" Family are Donna Culpepper, Tish Kronen Gluck, Helene Silverberg, and Mary Ann Whitten; and the friends who offered to share their homes even when it is a small studio: Aylin, Aysha, Candace, Erin, Hâle, Kıvanç, Oya, Patricia, Sezin, and Taymiya.

After my very intense two months' work in Athens, Latifa and Abd al-Hayy Weinman generously offered me their house in Taos during the completion of this book. The peace and quiet of New Mexico proved to be restorative and inspirational. I cannot thank them enough.

The manager of *Kahve Dünyası-Kabataş* Branch, a busy and popular coffee shop chain in Istanbul, offered their meeting room for us to assure privacy and first-rate sound recording with no background noise. Their service and coffee quality are matchless.

My family and friends supported my decision to stay in Berkeley despite the financial difficulties because they believed in me and in my commitment to document the lives of refugees. The displaced women had to face discrimination in the country they fled to and to hear the sad news pouring from their home countries on daily basis. They struggle with a tremendous amount of bureaucracy and people who either have no idea or very strong opinions about how to approach refugees or "outsiders" in general. I kept reminding my friends and family that my transition across countries is insignificant compared to what my participants have been going through. Each potential participant empowered me during this project and I am indebted to them. We walked the same or similar paths for some time and we all learned to travel light.

Preface

Journeys come in many forms: planned, unplanned, short, long, tiring, comforting, illuminating, legal, undocumented, on foot, by boat, with or without someone waiting at the other end. Syrian women have journeyed abroad in various combinations thereof since 2011. The nine women whose stories compose the main body of this book are still in transition in Canada, Germany, Greece, and Turkey, and I have no doubt that as life unfolds in its richness, their stories will develop further. The order of the stories is chronological for no particular reason—it could equally have been alphabetical according to the women's pseudonyms or age.

This book is a genuine firsthand account of Syrian women's lives before and after 2011, including their perspectives on a range of subjects which cannot be engaged with elsewhere in such detail and vivacity. This has been the longest and most challenging oral history and narrative inquiry project I have undertaken in my twenty year-long research and storytelling career; and it has also been the most rewarding. Immersed in the accessible, flowing language, the reader may not perceive the behind-the-scene challenges that the protagonist of each chapter presented to me as the story collector and writer. The same questions were asked of each but some shared more than the others. For the sake of authenticity, I have not shortened the interviews of the talkative ones or padded-out the reserved women's words to bring the chapters to a standard size.

It is July 22, 2016, and we are in the elegant ambiance of the City Club of San Francisco. After admiring the grand and controversial 1931 Diego Rivera fresco, Amy McCombs (professor emerita at the School of Journalism, University of Missouri) encourages me to expand my project to the maximum number of countries, if possible. We eye Calafia, the Spirit of California, whose right hand mines the Earth for its hidden treasures, while her left holds the treasures that grow above ground. I see clearly why the fresco is controversial, but I am glad to be in its presence and that Rivera created it. Likewise, the Syrian women's stories recounted here might also receive criticism. Nonetheless, I have gone ahead and done my best to avoid maiming the narratives. As a once middle-class, tame-looking former academic and now a practicing writer, might I risk being on the road to hell which is said to be paved with good intentions? I am grateful for Ms. McCombs' constructive conversation. The director of UC Berkeley's Center for Middle Eastern Studies, Emily Gottreich, encouraged me to apply for the Mellon Research Grant and I was able to travel to Sweden, Germany, and Canada to conduct the interviews.

This biographical enterprise differs from others on the market, or in the media, by virtue of the absence of drama and horror, and these are not a common link among the narrators. The tone and style stand in contrast to the work of investigative journalists and authors, such as Janine di Giovanni and Samar Yazbek, who have focused on the dramatic impact of war and conflict on women. Parts of their accounts are disturbingly tragic and graphic. Wendy Pearlman's collection of wartime testimonies from Syrians in *We Crossed a Bridge and It Trembled: Voices from Syria,* centers on the power of fragments of individual dialogue. What distinguishes my work from hers is that my co-participants' narratives span a lifetime, thus differing in length and content. Pearlman's respondents focus exclusively on the Assad regime's evils and the collective price citizens have been made to pay. The snippets are sharp and sometimes poetic in their brevity, and the number of personal narratives is greater. The German journalist Wolfgang Bauer's *Crossing the Sea: With Syrians on the Exodus to Europe* is another assembly of dramatic stories, including that of his four-day kidnapping by smugglers.

This book brings a real human face, not only to Syrian women's experiences, but to the experiences of refugee families everywhere. It contributes to life narrative scholarship through women's stories of the self in relation to memory, history, trauma, and reconciliation within familial, (inter) national and cultural contexts. The success of the narratives lies in their specificity, their simultaneous familiarity and novelty.

The relational element between the oral historian and co-participants requires an acknowledgment that the participants are always interpreting their pasts from their present vantage points. So, the historian actively attends to their stories accepting that *they* shape the stories. The relational responsibilities are understood as long-term—that is, as attentive to the participants' and oral historian's lives throughout the recording and writing processes, as well as their post-project lives as the future unfolds.

I am convinced that writing a book in an intellectually invigorating and international setting influences the outcome. That is why I am grateful to the Center for Middle Eastern Studies (CMES) for hosting me as a visiting scholar for 2016–2018. The position enabled me to use the Berkeley Library, attend lectures, and workshops, most of which were very inspiring. It also offered me several opportunities to share my work with students, colleagues, and the public. The Bay Area in general is a haven for any scholar due to the wealth of academic resources and the caliber of people living there. Two presentations in particular stand out.

The Native and the Refugee by Matt Peterson and Malek Rasamny is a multi-media project which profiles the spaces of Native American reservations and Palestinian refugee camps. Their goal is to encourage dialogue and a re-examination of the histories and structures that have produced the current situation for both communities. After attending Rasamny's talk at CMES, the significance of drawing mental maps by connecting temporal and spatial dots surfaced even more powerfully for me, making global solidarities more possible.

The second one took place at Books, Inc., in San Francisco in relation to an oral history project: *Crazy Horse: The Lakota Warrior's Life & Legacy*. One of the First Nation members in the audience told the author, William Matson, that if he hadn't come to the bookstore with the actual representatives of the Lakota, she would never have wasted her time or money for the book. Now that she witnessed an amiable bond between the oral historian/writer and Lakota members, she considered the work authentic and reliable. I pictured myself in a bookstore with some of the Syrian participants who shared their stories so that we too could display our alliance along with the book.

Buckets of tears were shed at some Bay Area events relating to Syrian refugees. The talks or documentaries were followed by organic vegetarian Middle Eastern delicacies, local coffee, and cookies. I knew from the beginning that my work would not present or claim reality in this manner, mostly because of possible outcomes such as vicarious trauma, which may become too unbearable. People leave not necessarily enlightened but being reminded once again that they are unable to do almost anything in the face of the atrocities. I am confident that the following stories will not trigger such feelings but will still leave the reader with a colorful potpourri of memorable scenes and emotions.

Nevertheless, I want readers to realize that we can become a refugee through any sudden turn of events. Iconic figures who have been formative and treasured parts of our lives, such as Rumi, Mother Mary, or the Dalai Lama, were also refugees. With this realization, we can begin to perceive their stories from a fuller perspective (not only as those of a poet of love; the mother of Jesus depicted on church windows and in icons; or a spectacled smiling old man in orange cloth whose quotations are shared out of context on social media). Likewise, we can begin to build connections with the lives of these nine women.

Scientists have discovered that cats' purring functions as a "natural healing mechanism," thereby inspiring the myth that they have nine lives. Wounded cats purr because it helps their bones and organs to heal and grow stronger. With the two-year long process of narrative inquiry (2016–2018), both the selected Syrian women and I discovered that story telling functions as natural healing too. We have grown stronger together and some have shared feelings of healing. Throughout, I was constantly asked by colleagues and friends, mainly in the U.S., whether I have been suffering from secondary trauma. Several books on healing were recommended to me, which were mainly new-age flavored self-help books. These people had the best intentions, but one thing they may have overlooked was the shared culture and geography that I and the nine Syrian co-participants were born and grew up in: the Middle East. There, the ancient tradition of *muhabbet* (friendly conversation) among women over tea or coffee existed long before therapy sessions or "girls' night outs" as a forum for recovery and healing. However, I am not willing to discard the concept of the bridge—an over-used yet favorite metaphor of mine. So please join me from wherever you are in this journey of crossing or building bridges between peoples and cultures. We live through such challenging times that we cannot afford abandoning bridges in our lives.

Introduction

Reciprocal Lifelines:
Representing Refugee Women

Syria, March 2011. Pro-democracy demonstrations shook the regime of Assad. A brutal and complex war fueled by political and sectarian divisions has claimed hundreds of thousands of people and created millions of refugees. The images of chaotic crowds, screaming people, rubble, and dead bodies either in Syria or on the shores of Turkey and Greece dominate global mainstream and social media. They trigger feelings of pity, revulsion, and estrangement among other emotional states, not leaving much room for the many untold stories of Syrians who can blend in, speak English, and maintain a life of their own as true but invisible survivors among us. Dealing with our own feelings at times like this can be challenging. One provision is doing our homework: Read, question, empathize, and humanize.

Turkey, February 2016. I am at an NGO office in the Esenler district of Istanbul, far from the neighborhood where I grew up, conducting my first interview in a clean and comfortable space reserved otherwise for refugee children. No one in that building could anticipate the disastrous events of the coming months, where hundreds of lives would be claimed by several terror attacks and the military coup attempt in Turkey. We still wanted to live in the illusion of safety, like most people do in Western Europe and North America. A new year, a novel project with women: I was made of a globe of emotions, ranging from excitement, anxiety, empowerment, and solidarity.

The United States, February 2018. I watch the snowflakes from the wide kitchen window where I am hosted by the Weinman family in Taos for completion of this book's journey. A unique dance by millions of snowflakes is on display, choreographed by an Invisible Designer, engulfing me in it, too. My gratefulness is growing every day for crossing paths with the Syrian women who agreed to share their life stories and now call me a lifelong friend.

Nine out of innumerable snowflakes dropped on the pages of this book. Their inimitable dance is relentless with no intermission. The Choreographer chose a stormy style with giant leaps from Syria to Canada, Sweden, Germany, Greece, and Turkey. The-would-be-tenth-flake faded away sooner than I could capture it, a gentle touch was hers, and with an apology too. How can one even imagine tending to a snowflake?

This volume offers accounts of nine selected women refugees from Syria who have been displaced and are in transition. My network in Istanbul made the initial contacts possible and I began reaching out to these genuine and fearless Syrian women. They don't know each other and are not related, except three of them who were connected only through Internet platforms such as Syrian interpreters' or humanitarian aid forums, thus they have not met in person.

Gender-specific roles of and expectations from girl-children, teenagers, married and single women, and mothers in Syria have been revealed during the process of recording these stories. However, these revelations remain complicated and need a cautious approach of intersectionality. The Syrian women's gender roles are enmeshed in the intersections of age, class, spirituality, geographical (dis)location, French colonialism, ethnicity, and citizenship in an authoritarian regime.

"Lifeline" as a metaphor has a bi-directional function. The women who shared their stories are not the only party who are excluded from power and knowledge resources. With the so-called post-truth politics, alternative facts, and the fake news sites that have been disproportionately circulated and consumed, the readers also need the narrators' lifelines. They should value and endeavor to find out about these unique individual stories to enrich their knowledge and understanding of Syrian life, culture, and growing up in Syria.

This volume does not focus on the tragedies of recent Syrian history while acknowledging the facts and the unacceptability of the incidents that have been on the global agenda since March 2011. The book is also an attempt to introduce novelties in oral history and narrative inquiry to students, scholars, activists, and the general reading public. The works on wars and conflicts by reporters can be alluring, but they are bound to be partial if not "perverse and lethal" when the elements of voyeurism and sacrificing the ordinary for juicy and tearful scenes are considered (Gagnon 155).

I had doubts about the participants' willingness to talk to me. I am not a therapist or a spiritual figure or a resettlement lawyer. Thus, I was ready to meet silence and accept it, too, having known, based on my previous work in oral history, that silence is not muteness. Certain silences can be eloquent and carry a lot of meanings. However, to my surprise, the participants were willing to talk. Our experiences have been empowering and that is why we keep in touch regardless of the country in which we find ourselves. Mobile phones help us connect and share fragments from our lives.

The life stories recounted herein are based on interviews conducted with nine women, aged 26 to 52, who are from Aleppo, Damascus, Daraa, Deir Ez-Zor, Homs, and Latakia. They are currently resettled in Canada, Germany, Greece, and Turkey. The chosen host countries had humanitarian asylum policies unlike the rest of the so-called democratic regimes.

Eight of the women had already moved twice, that is, after living in Turkey, they resettled in Canada, Germany or Greece. Except for three, the women co-participants crossed the borders to Europe and Canada legally. The stories capture childhood memories, early years of familial and formal education, the most significant people in their lives, religious beliefs and practices, marriage, having children (if applicable), and are arranged in chronological order.

Rose defines herself as a Kurdish Yazidi and an educator. She was born in Damascus but grew up in Aleppo. She has a BA in English literature. She is 52 and married with three children. The death of her older son was very traumatic, yet it allowed her to travel to Germany for his funeral, and that is where she sought asylum after two years in Turkey. Her daughter and son-in-law are also in Germany while her husband was stuck in Syria. Rose worked as a teacher in a Syrian school in Istanbul and later at an international NGO as an interpreter.

Lutfia, 47, is from Dara. She is married with three children and lives in Istanbul with her husband and her in-laws. She is a homemaker and has a degree from a vocational school in Aleppo. As a practicing Sunni-Muslim, she took the hijab after marriage, since her parents left the choice up to her, though her husband has more conservative views and a jealous nature. She wants to focus on Syrian children's education in Turkey.

Lutfia's interview was unique in that we were unable to talk directly. I went on a long search of interpreters based on certain criteria: an Arabic speaking-woman with sensibilities and experience with women and gender issues. Asma Khalifa, originally from Libya, proved to be the perfect interpreter. However, Asma and I had to leave Turkey in the summer of 2016. Unlike the other eight participants with whom I have direct and regular contact, getting even basic responses from Lutfia to the follow-up questions—after the interviews were complete—became a major hurdle. Overall, the three of us still claim to have immensely benefited from the experience.

Muzna is from Aleppo and was raised as a Sunni Muslim. She is a human rights activist with a BA in French linguistics. She has two brothers, each in a different country, and her parents live in Saudi Arabia. After living and working in Istanbul for a while, she received a grant from the Nobel Women's Initiative in Canada. Her asylum hearing in January 2017, around the same time that she turned 26, was successful. She began her MA in peace studies at Sherbrooke University in Quebec in fall 2017.

Sama is from Damascus and is 28 years old. She is a practicing Muslim with a degree in translation. After living in Lebanon and Turkey, Sama crossed the Aegean in 2015, on a boat with her parents and a younger sister. They reunited with her brothers in Germany and have been living there since. She is learning German very quickly and preparing for a new life with her Syrian fiancé, whom she met in Germany.

Emilia and her four older brothers were raised by a Muslim single mother in Homs. From 2011 on, she traveled by herself through Dubai, Jordan, Lebanon, and Yemen before arriving in Canada thanks to a scholarship by the World University Service of Canada in fall 2014. She is double majoring in psychology and political science. She likes dancing and having interesting conversations with people from different backgrounds. She is also 28 years old.

Zizinia is a dedicated single mother with two daughters. Although she has a degree in economics, she always wanted to study law and engage in restoring justice. She sought asylum in the U.S. in 2012, but her longing for her children and not knowing when that asylum would be granted caused her return and settle in Gaziantep, Turkey. She worked first at a Syrian NGO branch called Space of Hope, then in RMTeam. She is 38 years old.

Leila's family moved to Damascus from Deir Ez-Zor in 2008. She is from a middle-class, educated family with four children. She was studying environmental engineering in Aleppo when the war broke out. After her parents' friends lost a daughter on her commute to university, her parents were too concerned about her safety, so Leila wasn't allowed to continue her education at that time. Her transfer application to Istanbul University was successful and she has been studying there since 2013. She is 26 years old.

Sara is from Latakia and is the eldest of the four siblings born into a conservative Alawite family. She is 26, a self-proclaimed atheist and bisexual. She has a degree in pharmacy but her real interest lies in the fields of language and humanitarian aid. She left Syria in December 2015, first for Istanbul, then for Athens where she filed for asylum and found a job in a well-known international NGO after six months of homelessness.

Born in Aleppo in 1984, Bidaa grew up in a close-knit family with compassionate Sunni parents. She practiced law, with a specialization in intellectual property protection, for several years and has been an asylee in Athens since March 2016. As a devout Muslim, Bidaa makes an effort to dismantle stereotypes about Islam in Greece. She gives Arabic lessons to the children of expatriates from Arab countries and is learning Greek.

The main voices in this book belong to these nine Syrian women who generously shared their vantage point of growing up in Syria and how they found themselves amid demonstrations, war, and displacement before becoming refugees. Their stories are timely, their opinions and observations are as valid and important as any high-ranked politician. Their words are informative, and their narratives are presented in an accessible language that anyone can learn from and follow. They are empowered by their experiences and our process of recording their lives for this book, and they will seek to claim to power not only in their personal lives, but also in the public realm in the future. "Victim" is the last word that should be used to describe them.

These highly personal life narratives can be located in wider contexts of the socio-historical framework in which the co-participants live. This volume can thus be approached in two ways. One is locating them in a broader literature on forced displacement. These include, but are not limited to, economic and natural disaster–induced displacements. Secondly, this book can be embedded into the resettlement narratives of refugees from different geographical areas, time periods, class, education, and gender sensibilities.

The discussion of terminology and methodology is limited to the Introduction only. This is intentional since the first-hand and diverse accounts of women from Syria need to take precedence. Disseminating their words to an English-speaking audience with the hopes of dismantling some stereotypes and reclaiming women's own images and depictions of themselves is the ultimate goal. The same goal convinced the participants to take part in this book since all of them expressed frustration by being pigeonholed and discriminated against because of stereotypes and ignorance.

In the conclusion, converging and diverging themes are identified and analyzed in conjunction with (self)representations that arise from the narratives. The conclusion provides a realistic picture of the unexpected outcomes of displacement while uniting the nine narrators through threads of womanhood(s) and visions for a different future. It also suggests that having individual stories is essential to understanding how displacement can be managed and evaluated in a gender-equal manner.

The concept of "womanhood" and its use in the plural invites productive debates on the inclusion of "womanhood" into the mainstream language. The *Oxford English Dictionary* dates its use back to the late fourteenth century when Chaucer wrote on the "glory of womanhood" in *Canterbury Tales*. The word's present-day usage refers to the disposition, character, and qualities attributed to women, as well as the states of being a woman and the period following girlhood.

The plural form "womanhoods" is an intended political preference for the author as a gender and women's studies scholar, in order to draw attention to the distinctiveness and complexity of each woman's voice. It also evades the risk of sounding all-inclusive regarding the women in Syria.

"Co-participant" is selected to refer to the women who shared their stories with the author, but "narrator" is equally valid although it fails to recognize the reciprocity in the process. The label "author" can be enriched with the additional hyphenated designations among which are ethnographer, oral historian, recorder, and researcher. Susan Geiger, the author of the provocative article "What Is So Feminist About Women's Oral History?" argues for referring to the co-participant or the narrator as "the oral historian" (180). At the International Community of Artist Scholars Conference in San Francisco in February 2017, a scholar suggested that co-participants can also be named as "walking archives" with the intention of relocating the narrators within the discipline of history and challenging the concept of "archive." My tendency is not to allocate too much emphasis on terminology and to resist categorizations as much as possible.

Nevertheless, the genre question remains, regardless of how or where you picked up this book. I embrace the use of hybrid genres as a reader and writer, so I am glad academic circles are not as rigid as they used to be due to the hard-won feminist and anti-colonialist accomplishments in academia. The stories in the book are oral testimonies where the author rarely intervenes or inserts her feelings and observations to the main text. The length of the stories differs due to my choice to keep the authentic voices closest to the text and to reflect the unique characteristics of each individual.

My attempt to unravel and to translate the complexities of women's lives goes beyond boundaries of religion, nation, or ethnicity as well as genre. I don't contest that their realities are already lacerated by multiple displacements and memory lapses. Thus, at moments of despair and frustration while writing, I escaped to the idea that only fiction can restore some dimensions of truth and save some of my notes in a separate virtual folder. I consider myself fortunate to follow Svetlana Alexievich's path and reflect a polyphonic voice that documentary and literary prose can capture.

I share my admiration toward Ms. Alexievich and my concerns regarding representations of refugees with another female academic writer, Wendy Pearlman, who wrote *We Crossed a Bridge and It Trembled: Voices from Syria*. As a result, we both attempt to humanize displaced Syrian people, making room for diversity, and to portray individuals who are otherwise presented as security threats or victims. My addition is feminizing the discourse on refugees and migrants by privileging women's voices over that of others. Moreover, by prioritizing the female youth's voice, I "rejuvenate" the discourse, to borrow a popular term from the territory of cosmetics. Five out of these nine Syrian women are under thirty. In their place of origin, where I also grew up, being young and female means ranking the lowest in the cast. There are plenty of road signs which exemplify discrimination in the participants' narratives for the readers, some of which are reproduced even by the mothers among the respondents.

The list of queries was adapted from Robert Atkinson's *The Life Story Interview* (1998) and had around 120 questions. I began interviewing in Istanbul, moved to the U.S. in July 2016, traveled to Canada, Germany, Sweden, and Greece to conduct further interviews, which took place between March 2016 and January 2018. I transcribed the digital recordings myself, except for Lutfia's (my interpreter Asma Khalifa generously assumed both tasks) and Leila's (by Özge Balkaya) interviews. Sevil Şahutoğlu transcribed one-third of Zizinia's interview before passing it on to me. I argue that taking up transcribing affects the process of narrative composition positively on behalf of the author and strengthens her empathy and bonding experiences. I highly recommend it whenever possible.

Further concerns over women's agency, contextualization of their stories, criticism on physical distance between the participant and the writer, and the online follow-up clarification process can all be spared for analysis in journals and at conferences. Public lectures where the audience's questions probe and trigger several "behind the scenes" stories are among my favorite spaces to tackle these issues.

My respondent in Sweden pulled back due to several reasons, her time constraints being the major one. We hope there will come a time when we will complete her story. I miss her straightforward talk, sharp wit, advanced English, and soulful eyes which reflected wisdom. I always take the risk of someone's changing their mind in such a long-term and exhausting undertaking.

This book draws on data that were not explicitly intended for an academic audience. It is rather an exploration of ordinary upper-middle and middle-class Syrian women's lives and does not directly address political and socioeconomic dimensions of the Syrian conflict or propose robust policies in the conclusion. However, these testimonies reflect and expose certain demands, events, sentiments, and social aspects of being a woman in Syria through careful documentation of face-to-face interviews and online follow-up conversations.

My emphasis is on communication and sharing but this doesn't mean that extensive preparation work was not undertaken. On the contrary, I have spent several months studying Syria, its history, popular culture, classical songs, recipes, etcetera. I have even begun adding cardamom to my daily caffeine intake. Unlike many of the books about Syria published after 2011, this work doesn't allocate space for the history of Syria (ancient or contemporary) or provide a political background before 2011. There are plenty of valid resources for any English speaker who feels the need for history ranging from five-minute YouTube videos to full-fledged book chapters and online articles. The interviews focus around the past, present, and future, demanding hope, stimulating debates and highlighting the potential for change, especially on the roles of men and women.

Displacement and Islam: Catalyst for Transformation, a Daily Practice or an Identity Marker?

Another aspect of this volume lies in its suggestion to view displacement as a potential development and a catalyst for transformation, particularly for women who were expected, if not forced, into following certain gender roles in Syria. Displacement might enable intriguing shifts of empowerment for women due to their language abilities, their access to labor (even if it is contingent), and quality education. Muzna, Emilia, and Sara are perfect examples of young Syrian women in their mid-twenties whose spaces of liberty, education, and work were dramatically improved. Leila's case is also a story of emancipation, but a partial one since she is still in Turkey where the status "guest" differs from "refugee" and leaves Syrians in limbo.

My observation on young women's empowerment still needs a cautious approach due to the loss of women's networks and communities back home, which can be disempowering. Many Syrian women remain susceptible to human rights violations and further displacement, and all nine women experienced separation from their immediate family at some point during the past six years due to the war. Nevertheless, my work suggests a reconceptualization of women's empowerment amid societal and political transitions.

Technology allows for a strong and regular virtual network, which contributes to empowerment in general. All co-participants are avid users of social media and they regularly communicate with their families, friends, colleagues, and fellow activists through instant messaging apps. They constantly share images, text, and videos.

Smart phones are essential for the Syrian community. They are the lifelines and the umbilical cords to family members; they are owned by anonymous directors of numerous short films, which are presented at courts as evidence for the abuse and violence of the Assad regime. During my interviews, I lost count of the phones taken out of women's purses where they served as a source of myriad information and emotions. There are some anecdotal passages about these virtual communications in the book where I imagine the reader approvingly or affectionately smiling.

There is plenty of evidence in the narratives to demonstrate the complexity of the shifts in gender-roles during the process of resettlement. For instance, one needs to be vigilant of the attempts of increased control by male authority figures during the transition and resettlement processes, as in Sama's story. Her father's attitude changed and became stricter after the family arrived in Germany. He was concerned that his daughters might "go astray" being in a European country for the first time. After hours of conversation, he was able to relax a little yet hosted several potential in-laws in a row who were in search of a good Syrian bride in Germany.

Material impoverishment is the convergent consequence of war-ridden displacement, but the women refugees' range of coping and adaptation mechanisms, their connection to global networks to provide support and information to each other remain more than impressive. Not all the co-participants identify themselves as feminists or activists, adding diversity to the opinions expressed in their life narratives. Their varied belief spectrums range from being an atheist to being a practicing, head-covered, Muslim woman.

Finally, I intend to address the problematic representations of refugees from Muslim countries. The headscarf is not the only marker for a woman's religiosity in Islam. Nor does it mean that the person is a practicing Muslim. There are countless women in the Middle East who grew up Muslim and have adjusted their beliefs in individual doses, according to what they feel comfortable with. Most governments in the area are secular (Syria was/is one) so religion is allocated to the private sphere. It is not uncommon to meet young Muslim women who would go out at night in Western-style clothes, dance, drink, hang out with their boyfriends, and follow whatever they choose to follow when it comes to the practices of Islam. My random selection of the women in this book presents good evidence of this, and though it wasn't initially planned or anticipated, I am glad that several alternative representations and interpretations of Islam stand out in the text.

Being young and female pulls one down to the lowest ranks of society in certain countries, and Syria is among them. Consequently, making room for new and authentic voices becomes harder in the noisy agendas of world media. Moreover, cultural relativist biases against Syrian refugees cause hesitation in women when it comes to disclosing their stories, especially if the legal paperwork is still being shuffled around. Authenticity can be sacrificed for practicality when "strategic essentialism" is in use for a quicker access to legal status (Magnon 151).

The Invisible Survivors and the Question of Women's Agency

The degrees of women's agency in the narratives vary and allow room for each reader to have their own interpretation. Although the outcome of being a refugee for the majority is marginalization and deepened poverty, this may not always be the case, as several of my co-participants' stories reveal. By the virtue of their assets and status prior to resettlement, or due to their ambitious personalities, some refugees are able to improve their lives substantially after displacement.

The following nine individual accounts do not present the whole story, but they do provide intriguing glimpses into women's lives in Syria born between 1966 and 1992 and reveal several impacts of the Syrian conflict on an individual basis. I fully acknowledge Syria's complex religious and political landscape, and I chose to not interview Assad supporters or male refugees. The reader will notice that the degree of involvement in and sympathy for the "revolution" also differs in the book, as not all participants were among the street demonstrators.

Another choice I made was to bring "the invisible survivors" to the foreground among the displaced Syrians, as I have described my co-participants. The reason they are invisible is because they would "pass" in any European or North American city where they might be resettled. They speak English, their sartorial choices do not hint at any sign of religious affiliation except three, and they perform etiquette smoothly. As a result, six of the nine women are exposed to too many questions and taken as "native informants" by several curious or prejudiced host country nationals.

I edited the narratives for readability. I used pseudonyms throughout, including for family members and friends mentioned by the narrators, with one exception—Muzna Dureid insisted that I use her name. I am positive that her biography will one day be published in full, yet the mainstream definition of the genre requires her to grow older for it. Sara and Bidaa told me to use their first names but not their family names. The rest of the co-participants chose their own pseudonyms.

The experience of displacement has been hard on the co-participants but being free from the repressive attitude of the Assad regime, its officers, and institutions still proved a consolation. The rich details of personal narratives can do much to challenge stereotypes and they can function as correctives to the simplified accounts or images we are exposed to on a daily basis.

I have tried to do justice to the nine co-participant women, to their concerns and experiences but the resulting text is bound to be partial. Besides, it has been filtered through many layers since the time of our interviews were recorded, and it survived several negotiations. However, each participant knew from the beginning that they had the opportunity to intervene at any stage of the narrative inquiry process. They had access to the transcripts and were free to edit or remove any passage with which they did not feel comfortable.

The life story narratives are apt to expose the confusions, contradictions, and ambiguities that are part of our everyday experience and ourselves. The misleading and fragmented media representations of refugees in general, and Syrian women in particular, can be counterbalanced by oral history and life-writing techniques. In this sense, regardless of the terminology or categorization, recording and publishing a woman's life story is a valuable project which illustrates the need for a flexible and holistic perspective toward our understanding of refugees worldwide.

1

Rose's Story
On Names and Disguises

Early Years and Education

My name in Kurdish means rose. My mother named me after a special type of rose, that is found only in Syria, and known for its distinct scent. That is why I choose my pseudonym as Rose. One of my earliest memories is of the famous Mountain Quasioun or Jabal Qāsiyūn. You know it, right? [*She looks a bit disappointed when I shook my head*] There are two famous caves in it. The Cave of the Seven Sleepers and the Cave of Blood, where Cain killed Abel. Anyway, because we had no money, my parents could not buy any toys, but we were always allowed to climb up the hills of Quasioun to meet friends and have picnics. In fact, my mother told us to go there while she was busy doing house chores. It was very safe then and the air was so fresh.

I was born in Damascus on August 2, 1966. We were seven siblings, three girls and four boys, I was number four. There was no proper birth control at the time, you know? [*She laughs*] I remember feeling and knowing that I belonged to a poor family until I was twelve or so. We moved to Aleppo when I was ten. Everything changed, my friends, my surroundings. Although our neighbors were nice people, the school was difficult and unpleasant. There was gender segregation, the girls covered themselves, and the religion classes were compulsory. I was allowed to play only with girls. Before moving to Aleppo, I wasn't even aware of my gender. In Damascus, we were free; in Aleppo, the majority of people were conservative Sunni Muslims. Still, I didn't have to cover my hair then because I was a Yazidi.

My father began working in two jobs in Aleppo. He was a civil servant during the day and he worked as an accountant in a restaurant at nights. My mother was also working as a tailor from home. In time, we moved to a nicer and larger house with the money that they managed to save. During my teenager years, I felt comfortable, no longer poor.

My mother wasn't formally educated but demanded us to be accomplished students, and I had a good education. Now my children are having problems with schooling due to the war and moving two countries, but I will push them to complete their education in the same demanding manner that my mother had.

When I was only seven years old, I gathered all the girls in my neighborhood and told them, "now we are going to play a game. I am your teacher, you are my students." I remember the few steps that I climbed up with a stick in my hand and mimicked the teacher: A, B, C... My mom's uncle was a teacher and because of his profession, he was very much respected. I told myself that I should be like him. Education was and is very important to me.

I remember my first day of class in Damascus. My teacher loved me immediately, and do you know why? Because I read the Quran. I had acquired prayers by listening to the Muslim girls in my neighborhood who were reciting passages from the Quran. On the first day of school, the teacher asked whether anyone could read the Quran. I immediately raised my hand, curiously I was the only one, and I recited al-Fatiha. She complimented me and made the other students applaud me. Later in the week, she called me to the board and asked for calculations, among other things, and paid more compliments.

On another occasion, there was a substitute teacher, she asked the same question as soon as she walked in, "Who knows the Quran?" This time, I did not raise my hand, maybe because she was a stranger. She then randomly called on students. She beat the ones who could not recite the three lines on the board from the Quran. Those lines were not familiar to me either, but I said, "I may not know the words on the board but I *do* know the Quran. For example, I know al-Fatiha." She did not believe and called me a liar. I recited al-Fatiha and saved myself one more time. "Good job, go back to your seat now," was her final response. Now I am a teacher myself at a conservative school in Istanbul with a compulsory religion class. When some students cannot recite the prayers scheduled for the day, I ask them, "Do you know any other parts from the Quran?" If they can read some other lines, I accept it.

Kurdish is my mother tongue, I can also speak Arabic, English, and a little bit of French. Now, I am learning Turkish at a free language school near where I live. Despite the al-Fatiha story that I told you, my least favorite lesson was religion because it was compulsory. Learning to read the Quran was very difficult. Arabic in school was tough as well since it wasn't my mother tongue.

I began keeping a diary when I was ten as a result of moving to Aleppo in 1976, which upset me greatly. I jotted my feelings into a small notebook. The suffering triggered it. I have never been a regular diarist, but I returned to my diary a few years ago when people around me were dying or getting injured because of the war. At that time, we lived under constant threat of being bombed or killed. The notebook probably remained in our collapsed house in Aleppo. I have no idea.

The youngest of my four brothers was like my son, I took care of him as a baby. It is no wonder that even today, he considers me his mother. Before he got married, he asked my opinion and I ... well ... kind of chose his wife [*she laughs*]. He and his family are now in Greece. I talk to him often. All my siblings are college-educated. My husband's side of the family are deprived of education which makes it hard for me to deal with them. He prefers to ignore some of their biased commentaries but I can't. Educated people are more flexible and open to new ideas; at least, this is my assumption. Now that I think about it, the school where I am teaching is also conservative, although the teachers must have had formal education. We teach five hours per day, including Turkish. Sometimes we teach students songs and dances too, but it is not called music or art class because arts in general are considered inappropriate. This tells you the extent of conservatism in the schools which are set up for Syrian children in Turkey.

Forming Strength as a Girl-Child

I did not feel supported or encouraged as a child because my parents were very poor. We had no money to buy toys. In fact, my parents couldn't buy anything I wanted. Toys and games were denied to me. What I did instead was to make my own toys with leftover pieces of cloth that I spared from my mother's sewing. However, one of our rich Armenian neighbors had one daughter named Sony and they invited me to their beautiful house regularly. She had many toys to share with me and her mother baked and cooked nice food for us. I can't remember why Sony was all by herself and I was the only friend she received. Maybe she had an illness, or the family was overly protective of her.

I deeply felt at the time and know today that my father loved me a lot. He helped me with my homework in general and was the reason why math became my favorite topic in school. I was seven years old when one of my brothers pushed me out of the window and broke my arm. My father took me to the doctor and my arm was casted. I suddenly became the center of attention for my parents which made me very happy despite the trouble and the pain I had to go through. My father bought me a pair of red shoes. For a poor family like us, it was a big deal.

The most valuable inheritance that my father left me was his advice on being strong even under the most difficult circumstances. He repeated it many times, also just before he died when I was only 19 years old. He was 42, and my mother was 38. After our family disintegrated due to the war and we lost our house and other belongings, I often remember his advice and do my best to hold on to it. It is not easy.

I was on the running team until twelfth grade. Because I needed to prepare for the university entrance exams, I stopped. But it was also mainly due to my father, who did not like me to train with boys. I'd love to run today if I could; however, I have a cardiovascular disease. I went through a surgery and have a stent. It happened after I got married, but before the war.

During my teenager years, my father never allowed us to talk to boys, so we hung out with girls all the time. My brothers imitated him. Even today, when taking public transportation, I always choose the seat by a woman. I was afraid of my father's reactions, so I could not flirt or chat with any boy. When I was fourteen, I remember liking the son of a neighbor but not bringing myself to reveal it to even my closest friend Zozan. I only had daydreams, nothing more.

Intermingling of boys and girls was not approved in society but there were always some ways to get around or do things secretly. I remember one of my friends going out with a boy and telling me about it. This lasted for two years before he left her. The whole time, we kept it a secret.

One of my brother's friends in our neighborhood called him on the street one day and told him that he loved a girl whose picture was in his pocket. This memento was a proof of her love. My brother got very curious, but the guy refused to show the photograph to him, which drove my brother crazy because he got the idea that she must have been me! He came home, went right into the kitchen, took a knife, and told my mom: "I'm going to kill your daughter who gave her picture to a boy she loves." It was the most shocking thing, I can still see his face and the knife as if from an old film.

I hid behind my mother who saved me by immediately questioning my brother: "What are you talking about? Did you see the picture or not?" My brother shook his head, still grabbing the knife with anger. My mother continued, "Well then, let's go to your friend's house and see the picture." What happened afterward was what I heard from my mother. She told me that they knocked on the door, she introduced herself calmly and explained the situation to this boy whom I hesitate to call a "friend" of my brother even today. He said, "Look auntie, I swear God that she is not your daughter, but I cannot show you the picture, either. What if you know her or if you're friends with her mother, and she'll be in trouble then, won't she?" My mom promised the guy that she wouldn't tell it to a soul and he trusted her. When my mother and brother came back home, she said, "I've seen the picture with my own eyes, and it belongs to one of our neighbors' daughter." Things got settled, except that when my father came home that evening, I complained about my brother. His slander hurt me, and I got very scared by the sudden terror at home over nothing. My father shouted at him, and my brother couldn't utter a single word in return. My mother kept her promise to that rascal teenager and she never told us to whom the picture belonged.

My sister and I had our fun times as well. I remember hiding under a high sofa and making it my secret sanctuary, taking naps, and even stashing some snacks there. As a teenager, I wanted to have my space and not be available to my mother's orders all the time. I recall guests coming in the hot summer afternoons for a chat and I could see their legs dangling in front of my eyes. One time, the guests crowded the house and my mom kept looking for me, but I remained quiet. After they left the house, I disclosed my secret to my sister and she began hiding there as well. This continued for two years. It was like having your own house within the house. I must have sought some privacy this way, being the fourth of seven children in my family.

Another fun trick we played on my mother relates to reading the future from coffee drags, a common practice among women in Syria. My sister or I used to draw a ring inside the coffee cup with our fingertips or a nearby pen while the other one distracted her so that she didn't see the intervention. Then, she'd begin reading our cup and say, "Oh, I see a ring, you're getting engaged soon, my dear." We all laughed, studied our faces quizzically, but my sister and I laughed harder!

The hardest time I had as a teenager relates to a strong feeling of guilt which still lingers over my soul. My eldest sister was thirteen when my parents told her that she had to quit school to take care of housework. She got so upset and cried buckets. My grades were better than hers, so I continued my education. In fact, we both studied very hard, it wasn't fair to her. When I got my diploma, she was already married. She called to congratulate and told me that she was happy for me. My heart still aches from that phone call as I'm telling you the story.

I was emotionally very dependent on my sister. It might sound weird but when she got married, I was distraught; I could not get out of bed for a week. My mom took me to a doctor. I was very angry and kept asking, "Why did she have to leave me?" She was like a second mother to me, and I am sure she still loves me in her own ways.

When it was time for me to enroll university, my GPA allowed me for

English Literature program, to which I was looking forward. However, my father wanted me to study medicine and initially sounded upset that my grades didn't qualify me for the program. I enjoyed studying literature, and in time, my father accepted my choice and even acted out with me during our imaginary living in Britain. London has been my dream city (even today!) so he would ask me to tell me in English how it was like to visit the city and so on. We dreamed about visiting London one day, but he died too young.

I should mention two of my professors who influenced me positively: Professor Faiz and Professor Arami. All students were afraid of Faiz since we felt his eyes on each one of us even in a large lecture hall. He shouted at us loudly when he wanted absolute silence. He was originally from Egypt but because he rarely spoke Arabic during the lectures, one couldn't tell this from his dialect. If you studied hard, you could actually get the grade that you deserved, whereas with the other professors, you couldn't get above a certain mark no matter how perfectly you performed in the exams. I took Poetry (1st year), Novel (2nd year), and Shakespeare (3rd year) courses from him and really enjoyed his lectures. I have heard that he is still alive but moved back to Egypt.

Mohammed Arami was originally from Damascus, but he studied in Britain. He was very critical of Western cultures and colonialism, and he told us a story which stands out vividly in my memory: One day, he was sitting at the student cafeteria with his friends from the same department. They spread an old newspaper on the table to eat on it or something like that, and noticed some news about Arabs, which were reported very negatively. The British students made several bad jokes about Arabs as if Arami were not there. It was an awkward situation. He didn't start an argument or even comment on it, but he never forgot the incident, either. Did they accept him as one of them, that is, a British? He told us not to be ashamed of being an Arab or Syrian when we traveled abroad.

I left the house only when I got married, not while I was studying. In Syria, you bring shame on your family if you leave your house as a young single girl. I have a relative in France who is a doctor. I introduced him to a Syrian Yazidi girl, who lives in Paris by herself. I told her that if my relative learns that she lives by herself, there is no chance that he'll marry her! Instead, I made up a white lie that she lives with her sisters and one brother. They will soon get married, they communicate regularly. He is in Istanbul now and we will see if he can go to France since there are some bureaucratic difficulties.

Rose's Criteria for the Right Man: Marriage

I met my husband through my sister. I was only fifteen, but I didn't know then that he would become my husband. Abdulah arrived in Aleppo to study civil engineering and rented a place next to my sister. I was on the balcony when he saw me for the first time. I had long hair and was dressed up because I was visiting my sister and her family. He suddenly realized that he ran out of bread and knocked on my sister's door to ask for a few slices! He also enquired who I was. He kept me on his mind and once he graduated from the university, he called my sister to see if I was still single. Indeed, I was! My sister agreed to our communication.

However, my cousin had already asked for my hand and my mother was okay with it. I wanted to marry Abdulah because he was an educated man with knowledge of different cultures and languages. My cousin was rich but uneducated. This was the argument I used to convince my mother, with which she reluctantly agreed. I also played a small game with my cousin. Living with the in-laws was a common and expected practice at the time but I demanded a separate house whose deed would be under my name. My aunt did not like the idea at all, so my plan actually worked. On the day of the wedding, my cousin came by the door and began disturbing the setting. I was so scared that day, I thought something would happen but did not. I believe having my four brothers in the crowd helped! However, my cousin never talked to me afterward. I heard that he died recently and was buried in Istanbul.

When I got married, I didn't know how to run a house. My mother didn't let me do any house chores so that I could focus on my studies. My husband used to tease me a lot: "Why did I take you as my wife? You don't know anything!" I remember having a genuine interest and curiosity in cooking as a child, but my mother never let me experiment even. I taught my daughter everything before she got married because I had difficult time adjusting to housework.

The first two years of my marriage were the most difficult due to some financial problems. My husband worked in two jobs and I was teaching full time with no childcare support. However, I couldn't complain to anyone, especially to my mother since I knew her response ("you should have gotten married to your cousin!"). In time, things got better. Twenty-three years passed as a couple.

The last house we owned in Aleppo was near a large park in a nice neighborhood, which today is in ruins. It was on the second floor of a four-story building with three bedrooms and one corridor. My husband and I furnished it, we bought everything new and the best quality. The color of the cupboards in the kitchen was green olive color mixed with black. There was a big shopping mall nearby. At weekends, I used to drive to an even larger one. We used to go to Latakia for swimming. Do you know that I learned swimming in my late twenties, after I got married? I took private lessons, and I remember, I almost got drowned once! My daughter was also in the same pool with no help because she thought I was just joking, acting like I was drowning. But when I got the hang of it, I fell in love with swimming! I miss it now, I can't even remember the last time I swam.

We lost one car already due to bombs and had to buy another. My husband sold this car recently; he didn't want to drive it any longer [*Rose got very upset, so I asked about her music preferences to distract her*]. Oh, I love listening to the songs of Fairuz and Umm Kulthum especially when I am cooking and cleaning. If the radio plays one of Umm Kulthum's songs, I wait until she finishes even when I know that I'll be late to wherever I am heading to afterward. She reminds me of my childhood memories and time stops for me with her songs. I also find Warda el Jezeiria remarkable. I was nine years old when I listened to Warda for the first time and fell in love with her voice. I listen to Fairuz during the morning chores, and Umm Kulthum in the evenings.

Abdulah and my daughter don't like these wonderful singers. My husband doesn't listen to Arabic songs in general mainly due to our Kurdish origins but Fairuz, Umm Kulthum, and Warda el Jezeiria are amazing. Once we were driving to his village and I inserted a cassette into the car's music player. He stopped the car and told me that he was worried about the locals' reaction if they heard Arabic music. Like him, they considered Arabic as the language of the oppressor. We listened to the songs that I chose until we got close to the village and then changed the music. Guess what he does nowadays when we talk on the phone? He makes me listen to the Arabic songs that I like if they are on the radio.

Do I have other hobbies or favorite writers? Not, really. I don't read much anymore but when I was at college, I used to admire the works of Shakespeare and Ihsan Abd el Kaddus, an Egyptian novelist and journalist. Among the women, I can only think of Colette Khoury, who is a brave Christian Syrian journalist. I bet she has good friends at the top of the government though, otherwise, she would long be in jail.

On Practices and Interpretations of Being a Yazidi and Discrimination at Work in Syria

In all these years in Aleppo, we could never say we were Yazidis. We learned the basics of our beliefs in secret through our parents. We pray, we fast, and some Yazidis go to pilgrimage in Lalish (Iraq) if they can afford it. We have two religious festivals, one in winter, one in summer, during which we visit family members, but the largest festival of the year is in October called *Jamaiyya*. It means the Feast of the Assembly, when all who can afford travel to Lalish and fulfill their religious duty. We believe that the Seven Angels gather at Lalish at this time to decide the course of the forthcoming year. On the fifth day, a bull is sacrificed to Sheikh Shems, one of the Seven Angels. On the seventh, a ceremonial bier of Sheikh Adi is made and decorated with cloths. *Jamaiyya* is an important occasion also in our social life, where friendships can be built, and disputes can be resolved. Families picnic in the valley of Lalish, catching up with old friends and meeting new ones. A perfect place for future couples to meet as well! There is a holiday atmosphere as well as solemn religious rituals where you feel the need to be quiet and respectful, so it is a nice combination.

During these festivals, special food is prepared and shared. We eat desserts, meatballs, and *sambusak*, a bite-sized savory turnover. Our family was never wealthy enough to visit Lalish, but we used to sacrifice chicken and prepare a feast out of it. The idea is to spill blood and if you are rich, you can sacrifice sheep or bull. As a ritualistic demonstration of respect, we kiss the hands of old people, similar to Muslims' *bayram* traditions. You hold the person's hand whose palm is facing down, kiss it, and touch it to your forehead, bowing down your head.

I believe in one God and Tawûsê Angel, which is in the form of a peacock. If I felt safe, I'd wear a pendant which symbolizes that I am a Yazidi, just like Christians' wearing a cross. My children don't know much about Yazidi traditions. In fact, when my older son made it to Germany, for the first time in his life, he can reveal that he is a Yazidi. Because of the missionaries approaching him on daily basis, he developed an interest toward his religion and began asking questions about it. I told him to pose these questions to his father since I felt inadequate about answering them. I can't even imagine a place where we as Yazidis can discuss or inform people about our history and traditions. There is one Yazidi school in Iraq to my knowledge, but we don't have any in Syria. In Germany, I hear that there are several schools and my older son can learn about his own culture and religion in freedom now.

Are there other Yazidi traditions or rituals that can't be found in the books? Well, I can tell you about a magic recipe, but it might be a Kurdish or a regional ancient practice. I can't even spell it since I have never seen it in writing. We call it *peixun*.

This mix is made up of pounded dried beans, pumpkin seeds, lentils, and salt among some other powdered seeds that I am not sure about. You pound them all together with pestle and mortar. According to our belief, if you consume some of this powder on the night of St. Valentine, your future partner will visit you in a dream. It happened both to my mother and to me, so we strongly believe in this. In her dream, my mother went to my father's village and drank from the fountain, which was interpreted the next morning as the place where she would go as a bride and live.

When I tested the powder as a teenager one night, I dreamed that my friend and I were in a big cafeteria at night time, which would be impossible in real life. A man who had a mole on one cheek was staring at us, so I asked my friend who the person was. She replied that he was an engineer, either studied or worked in Russia. I woke up and shared the dream with my mom. Two years later, my sister called me and told me about this engineer who was interested in meeting me. It was my husband and he had a mole on one cheek. He studied and did some business in Russia as I learned later. Wouldn't you believe in the power of *peixun* if you were me?

You can consume it anytime, but it is better to have an intention when you take it and then go to sleep. We believe that it works best if you practice it on Wednesdays, the holy day for Yazidis. I recently got some from a Kurdish neighbor in Istanbul. I was surprised to see her preparing this huge pot of *peixun*. I immediately set an intention about my daughter and had some before I went to sleep.

In my dream, my sister, daughter, and I were sitting in a room. There was a small creature about which we speculated. I told them that it was probably a fly but could have been a very small bird as well. If it were a fly, it is not a good sign. However, as soon as my daughter held it, the creature turned into a peacock, a wonderful symbol for Yazidis. At the time of my dream, she and her husband were still wandering on foot around the borders of Europe and were denied entry to Germany a few times. After the dream, I was so relieved because I knew that they would be admitted soon, and they were.

Being a Yazidi in Syria has become extremely dangerous after ISIS got empowered and took hold of certain territories in the country. However, non–Alawites have always suffered from discrimination during both the father and the son Assad's reign. I chose to remain apolitical in all those years and didn't want to get into trouble. For instance, speaking Kurdish in public was banned, but I told my family and friends, "it's okay, we can talk at home as much as we want, don't make it a big deal." Abdulah was denied promotion several times; yet, he was asked to accompany to many engineer teams during most business trips. Both of us knew that it was to take advantage of his education and experiences. He wrote numerous project proposals and evaluation reports, but his name was never mentioned in them, only the Alawite staff's names were printed. Can you believe it? Until the first year of the war, he stayed at his position as a civil servant despite decades of discrimination at work but then he quit. He lives in Afrin (as of spring 2016) with his sister and takes care of the olive groves.

Once on a Newrouz day in Aleppo, my colleague and I wanted to attend the street celebrations after school. The director didn't give us the day off although she knew that we were of Kurdish origin. We left the school building at noon and I was hoping to celebrate but then saw many soldiers who began insulting us with animal names (dogs, monkeys etc.) I suddenly got so afraid and had a bad taste in my mouth so instead of joining the street celebrations, I went directly home and told my family to stay at home.

One day, ISIS militants stopped the public bus that my husband and I were in. I was the only woman in it. All passengers were pushed out. I was so afraid that my whole body got shaky. They'd kill us if they learned we were Yazidis. ISIS members don't want any woman in public, plus, they hate Kurds. We had a mixed crowd of passengers. The driver said we were all Arabs. I made up a village name so they couldn't guess that we were Kurdish. We waited and waited for four long hours. Finally, the Amir, their leader, arrived and asked me why I was out. I told him that my father was very sick, and my family asked me to be with him blab blah…. They did not check our IDs. The driver was reproached for commuting on that route. I will never forget that day. We barely escaped execution.

Children, My Gems…

My older son Riyad has given me the most headache since I was pregnant with him back in 1997. On November 5, 2013, he was hit in the head during an airstrike in front of our apartment and severely injured. He is the reason why I decided to leave the country as soon as he could walk, leaving my husband and some of my best friends behind.

Born in 1993, my daughter Farah is blond with green eyes, contrasting the darker complexion of her two siblings. In her early twenties, Farah fell in love and got married when her university education was left incomplete due to the war. Her husband worked for the municipality as a civil servant that had nothing to do with his philosophy degree. They are in Munich as of August 2017 and trying to settle in after a long journey from Istanbul across Europe. As a staunch supporter of formal education, I want my daughter to get a diploma eventually. I was devastated when she had a miscarriage but maybe it was for the better considering her interrupted education.

My youngest, Mohand, is a hard-working teenager and manages to receive the highest grades and compliments from his teachers despite his obsession with football. He worked at a textile shop for pocket money while attending high school in Istanbul. Like all Syrian workers there, he was underpaid, around 140$ a month, but he did everything well regardless. It is his nature so when he wanted to quit to prepare for his final exams, the owner insisted that he stay. Mohand graduated high school in June 2017 and his Turkish test score was 96 out 100! I do my best to keep an eye on each one of my core family member thanks to the smart phones: I talk to my husband who lives with his sister's family in Syria, I check his health, ask occasionally about our deserted olive grove, which once gave us hope and healthy produce. Then I talk to Riyad, who is under medical surveillance but volunteers as an interpreter at a camp near Frankfurt. It is followed by another call to my daughter in Munich.

The most special gift I have ever received was on a Mother's Day when Abdulah called and told me not to cook for the night. I completely forgot that it was the Mother's Day because I was very exhausted with the children. They wore me out when they were little, and I had no child support. He took me out to dinner and gave me a gold ring with two hearts. I was so surprised! Marrying him was the most important decision of my life and definitely a turning point.

Another unforgettable memory is when I was pregnant with my second child. I failed to get pregnant for four years, and finally accepted the situation after visiting a few doctors. Then I got pregnant! Not surprisingly, we were paying utmost attention so that we didn't lose the baby. On that day, I was six-months pregnant and doing laundry. Our old washing machine made a horrible noise while wringing the clothes and it moved around. Right at that moment, Abdulah came and told me to stay where I was. He then began talking about some daily anecdote, something insignificant. Afterward, I learned that there was an earthquake and he rushed to see how I was doing. When he found me at our regular mini-earthquake zone, he successfully hid it from me just by talking and keeping me there. The next thing I remember was our neighbor's knocking on the door and telling us to leave the house immediately. I already had my bag ready by the door because of my pregnancy but the earthquake was gone!

My only dream is to see my family united [*She sighs*]. I remember some special days that we used to celebrate such as our birthdays or the March 8 dinners with my husband. Abdulah never failed to take me out on International Women's Day, which is an official holiday in Syria. This year, I don't feel like celebrating the mid–April feast that all Yazidis consider very significant, which is on *Charshema Sor* (Red Wednesday). This, however, is definitely not a holiday in Syria. The day commemorates Peacock Angel/ *Tawûsê Melek*'s descent to the earth to spread his dazzling wings in order to bless the earth with peace and fertility. It is considered the oldest surviving feast in Mesopotamia.

My older son Riyad shares everything with me. He has always been the closest to me among my three children. Not long after his arrival to Germany, a Syrian Sunni woman in the refugee camp that he was living asked him if he would like to take her daughter as his wife. She probably saw that he was a decent and helpful young man with good manners, and as a mother who is concerned about her daughter's wellbeing in a foreign country, maybe her proposal was understandable. Riyad wasn't sure how to respond so he said that he'd consult his family. When I heard the news, I told him that I don't approve of a Sunni Muslim girl as a bride and rather see him marry a German woman in the future if he can't meet a Yazidi. Thus, he told the mother that he was too young to marry and had plans to learn German and start university in Germany. After he graduates and is able to make a living, then he'd consider marriage and so on.

My Interpretations of Spirituality

Religion should not be a driving force to judge people. First and foremost, I believe in one God, so I don't separate people as Muslim or Christian. I distinguish them by their characters such as honest, good, compassionate, and full of love. This is my criteria for spirituality. I define myself based on my good deeds. When I die, I hope that people will remember me as a good person. That's all I want. Everywhere I go, this is already what happened, and I am not telling you this to show off. If you meet any of my colleagues—and I worked in many schools—all of them will comment positively about me. If I am a good person, God will protect me.

I also believe that things happen for a reason, we humans just don't know why it is happening at the time. I can give you some examples from my life. In our prosperous days, Abdulah and I helped many people who were in need, be them our relatives or his workers. When he was diagnosed with a heart condition, the doctor told me, "I cannot explain how your husband managed to stay alive with these clogged veins, it is a miracle. He should be dead by now." I told the doctor that Abdulah is a very good person, he has helped many people, so God kept him alive. They immediately operated on him, and thank God, it went well, and he is still with us today. Your good deeds follow you wherever you go. Nevertheless, I always carry a blue bead against evil eyes, and make my children to carry one with them too. Some people may consider it superstitious but the protection against envious gazes exists in many cultures and I fear their malicious power.

At the beginning of the war in 2011, all rich families who could afford a human trafficker immediately began sending their children abroad. Each person cost fifteen thousand euros. When I heard the rate, I was shocked and very upset, thinking that we could never afford leaving Syria even if things got worse. But when the bomb-incident happened and my son Riyad got severely injured in the head, sending him to Germany was down to only one thousand euros. He went through Bulgaria with a trafficker.

We had a neighbor here in Istanbul whose application for asylum got accepted much ahead of the other applicants because he had only one kidney and his condition was deteriorating. See how having one kidney can take you to Europe legally? My husband's health is also getting worse every day due to a hemoglobin disease and he needs blood. Maybe similar to our neighbor, he too will get a special paper and leave Syria. I don't know if these stories are related to your question about spirituality, but I somehow connect them.

I just remembered another incident of serendipity. Something which upset me at the time miraculously turned out to be to my advantage later on. Although I was born in Damascus, my father registered me in Aleppo for practical reasons whose details I can't even remember. I made it an issue and asked my father why he did not properly register me in my favorite city of Syria. Many years later, when I graduated from university and wanted to get a teaching position, I went to fill out the forms, but the person in charge told me that they only accepted the applicants whose city of birth was Aleppo.

I got very upset, I really needed the job, so I left, only to remember that according to my official records I was born in Aleppo! I can't forget the guy's face when I showed up again and applied for the position. I prayed for my father's soul when I got the job. It might sound insignificant, but this was a very crucial detail in my life, so I want to include it as an example to my spirituality.

I think when one believes in God, that is where one can gather the power from or seek refuge in. After I lost my father and later my mother, I was grateful to the extended family members who came to support us. After all, it was a good thing that God brought us to Aleppo even though as a child I had felt so desperate to move out of Damascus.

When Abdulah had a heart surgery, a similar inner strength took hold of me. I kept thinking, "He is going to be all right because he is a good person." However, when my son got hit in the head and almost died, that incident was harder to accept. I was out of my mind. I wanted to kill whoever were responsible for dropping that bomb. I rebelled strongly at the time. He was so young and innocent.

For three weeks in November 2013, I didn't leave the intensive care room at the hospital. I didn't even take a shower. I slept on the cold floor while it was snowing outside. I must have been a real mess. Nobody could console or convince me to leave my son. I don't have a clear memory of those weeks, but I do remember helping with anything that I could at the hospital, mopping the floors, assisting the nurses, etcetera. They were short of staff since too many wounded people were constantly brought to the hospital. I was told later that the doctors monitored me from the small camera that was installed in the intensive care room whereas I thought that they had forgotten me because of the constant chaos at the hospital. It took a full month before Riyad gained consciousness and opened his eyes. As he got better, I slowly turned to God, thinking that maybe it was a test, and I was gradually passing it. I promised God that I would volunteer at the hospital for another full week after my son's condition improved.

You should have witnessed the day Riyad opened his eyes and stared at us, and the following six or seven days. He was all in bandages and there was a tube running through his throat. When I pressed it, he would try to utter some words. However, he couldn't recognize me on the day when he finally opened his eyes. He gave me that long, blank stare. Abdulah and I rushed to the doctor in panic who told us that Riyad might need some more days before he could perceive his surrounding and remember people. He also advised not to ask any questions, probably because it might confuse Riyad, or who knows? The brain is a mysterious organ. He had a major brain trauma, so we are so lucky to have him back. A week later, we asked him who we were, and he knew the answer!

On Regrets and a Lebanese Refugee Neighbor

So many things that are beyond our imagination have happened since March 2011. But here I am in Istanbul and life goes on. Sometimes I meet very depressed people who think that they are going through a lot. I tell them to be strong, just like my father used to remind us when he was alive. These people need to seek help, get out of their house, or bed, and talk to other people. You have to face your problems. If you don't do it who else is going to do for you? Time heals everything, it is true. Gathering your power back might take time and it might be slower than you would like it to be, but it will come.

I don't have many regrets in life but a few of them come to surface when I talk to my children on the phone. For example, I find myself telling my daughter repeatedly that they should not bother saving money or overwork themselves like Abdulah and I did for many years. What happened now? We have nothing. I live in a shanty town where I don't feel safe or welcomed. One day, I left the laundry hanging outside and went to the supermarket. When I got back in less than an hour, my coat was stolen! One night, I saw a dark figure right by the window who cut the electricity lines. Why would you do such a thing? Clearly, burglars were getting ready to break into the houses in the neighborhood. What kind of city is this?

As for the neighbors, I am clearly excluded from all their activities for some reason. I see them sitting outside their houses, drink tea together, have conversations, and they never invite me. No, it's not the language issue, it must be something else. I can carry a conversation in Turkish. Besides, I have a neighbor who is Kurdish, born and raised in Turkey, and she knows that we share the same mother tongue, but she doesn't even greet me. The landlady comes once a month only to take the rent and never asks about our wellbeing or bothers to exchange a few nice words of greetings. There was a wedding ceremony last week in the neighborhood and I was not invited. Not that I care about attending weddings but in Syria, this wouldn't have happened. People were friendlier there. It is basic courtesy toward the new comers that I am missing here in Şahintepe.[1]

My husband worked so hard during the first years of my daughter's birth that he didn't even realize how or when she reached puberty. I lost the most valuable gifts from my husband to the human traffickers. Here is my advice, "Don't save money, don't buy houses, enjoy the present moment." But my daughter doesn't agree with me. Now they are in Germany and will work very hard to build a new life for themselves. I can only hope that they won't miss life, the precious moments that are impossible to get back.

I also wish that I treated my mother better. Because of her controlling personality and weak nerves, I didn't want to have her around but after my daughter got married, I began to understand my mother better. However, she is no longer around. One more regret that I can think of relates to my husband's father when he was sick. I remember asking Abdulah why it was always us helping out since he was not the only son in the family. I wish I didn't say that at all and I am so glad that he continued helping his father fully despite my criticism.

When I get really upset, I fall sick and am no good for anyone. I already told you that I stayed in bed for a week when my closest sister got married and left home. I also got sick when my daughter lost her baby when she was two months pregnant in 2015. I blamed her husband for making her work and stopped talking to him for a while, but we made up eventually. I can't afford losing my family any more.

Life turns out. I remember a Lebanese woman who escaped the war and became my neighbor in 1980. She used to come to my house regularly and cry a lot when she told me how she arrived in Syria with one small luggage. She was from a rich family who once owned factories and many cars. I felt so sorry for her at the time. It didn't cross my mind that one day I'd have to leave my country exactly the way that she did. With one small bag!

Building a family and having children are the most important things in my life. I remember after my mother's funeral, I came home and told my husband that I wanted to have six children. He thought I was still in shock because of my mother's death so he teased me gently: "My soul, you can't even take care of our only daughter, how can you possibly deal with six children?" I told him that when I looked around the crowd gathered at the cemetery, I realized how my mother brought us all together and revived our family bonds. I felt good about it and wished the same for myself. I also recognized how family-oriented I was as a woman. I can't think of a life without children. Well, we stopped at three, but I am proud and happy to have them.

It is hard to believe the kind of troubles that a human being can handle and still have a smile or crack jokes, isn't it? We wasted so much money to flee the country with my injured son Riyad who had a difficult time walking among the thorny bushes in the middle of the night. At least he had boots. I had bad shoes with terrible soles, which were covered with thick mud. I threw them away as soon as we crossed to Turkey.

One of my former students in Aleppo approached me the other day and introduced herself. Her son is in my class in Istanbul now. I mentioned her here because she said that she hardly recognized me. I used to take care of myself, dye my hair, put on make-up, and do stuff that women spend time to look nice, you know. A few weeks ago, one friend came home with her toiletry bag and claimed that some make-up would cheer me up, but I refused to put on any. I remembered Abdulah's jokes about my dressing up for the others, not for him because I was very casual at home. I guess such things like stylish clothing or cosmetics lost their importance a while ago. My husband can't cross the border illegally; his health is too fragile for such an escape. I don't want to make myself attractive for other people.

The Author's Touch

April 16, 2016, marked our last face-to-face interview in Istanbul. After the recording was completed, Rose and I took a walk by the sea and chatted freely. Then, we sat down at a simple tea-garden with ugly plastic chairs and spectacular views of the Marmara Sea, ferries, and the seagulls. After we ordered tea, Rose took out the tabbouleh, a delicious bulgur salad that she prepared at home. She also dug out a gift for me from her large purse, a beautiful long scarf in different tones of blue and silver. "Thank you so much Ozlem," she hugged me and kissed my cheeks twice as is the tradition in Syria and Turkey. I laughed and wrapped the shawl around my neck with an exaggerated gesture of a movie star to cover my emotions. From where we nested, we could see the historic peninsula, the iconic Topkapı Palace and the rest. I asked her whether she likes that area. She said she has never been there, "I don't want to visit those places by myself. My son doesn't like to hang out with me. Maybe, with my husband, one day...."

The hope was still there then, and I was glad to feel it in her words. Hope needs to be there, not just for Rose but for all of us, who are going through yet another shameful period in history. My effort was to keep Rose's voice distinct like the unique scent the rose bush in Damascus is known for and pass her story along because she wants me to.

However...

April 14, 2017: One year from that lovely day, I received the news from an activist friend who introduced us that Rose lost her son Riyad in Germany due to the complications resulting from his brain trauma. I sent her several messages, reminding of her own words on being strong and keeping the hope. However, there was no response. Rose's profile photo was changed from a peacock to pitch black, and I was told by our common friend that she was inconsolable. She finally broke her silence and sent me a voice message through WhatsApp: "I'm at the airport now, I am going to Germany to bury my son." The words burned my ears, her voice was muffled, almost unrecognizable. I mumbled some phrases of consolation in English before calling our common friend who gave me the news to learn more. An exceptional visa was issued for Rose by the German Consulate and that's how she was able to travel to Germany to attend the funeral.

April 2018: Rose lives in Saarbrucken, is learning German. Her younger son Mohand crossed the border illegally in January and joined her in Germany. This reunification was something she became obsessed about after Riyad. The truth is she is barely alive after Riyad's death. She sent me two more voice messages where the sentences were left incomplete and choked with tears. Her husband Abdulah had to be relocated from Afrin with the rest of his family in Syria after the Turkish military operation "Olive Branch" began in mid–January 2018. His health deteriorated and finding blood has become impossible in Syria according to Rose's messages sent on March 21, 2018, in response to my Newrouz wishes. The hope is still lingering somewhere else.

2

Lutfia's Story
Amidst the Personal
and the Political Conflicts

Growing Up as a Girl in a Conservative Town:
My Father Was My Hero

I was born in 1971 in Daraa as the oldest of four daughters, which was considered quite an unfortunate event for many families in Syria. However, my father never discriminated against his daughters. He was the most compassionate human on earth for me. My aunts would ask him, "Why do you value your daughters so much?" almost in a curious manner, and he would say, "They are my girls, my flesh and blood."

My mother was also very kind and compassionate. She is in Canada now, and we talk twice or three times a day. She was in Egypt first, as she and my two brothers were enrolled in an asylum-seeking program. Only one of my brothers, however, got accepted to Canada so my mother left with him and his immediate family. Imagine a new life, culture, and language at the age of sixty-five, but she is doing fine, thank Allah. She told me the other day that she was the most successful student in her English class.

One memory from my childhood years relates to the kindness of my father and how punishing a child can have its alternatives. My mother left the house for a visit to the neighbor, and I fought with my sisters and beat them for whatever reason. When my sisters told my mother what had happened, she called my father and asked him to punish me. My father never beat us. But this time my mother was insistent that he should beat me, so he gave in finally and said: "Okay, I will do it," and he took me to his room. He opened the wardrobe and gave me a watch to embarrass me with his kindness and by his being so good to me. I felt very ashamed of beating up my siblings and never did it again.

When we were teenagers, my father also displayed a completely different attitude from my friends' parents regarding relationships with the opposite sex. Being in the security forces, he heard too many stories of girls' getting severely punished or killed due to clandestine liaisons and rumors. He wanted to protect us from all these risks. He told us that if there were boys who we liked or fell in love with, we should let him know. My father wanted to meet them in person and ask questions to learn more about their characters and family. "Nothing behind my back," he said, and I still admire him for this, while trying to practice it with my own children.

My father is my hero. He taught us how to swim, drive a car, ride a bicycle, and do CPR. He taught us everything in this life. I made sure to pass these skills on to my own children. He gave us more freedom than any of the families that I have known. Before I got married, I wasn't wearing a headscarf, although my mother wanted me to cover. My father left it to our decision, and I chose not to. At my parents' house, I was treated like an adult and given several responsibilities. My opinions mattered then. However, my husband has not followed those practices in our house, which was so difficult to swallow, because I feel like ... we shared the house, but I would learn his decisions from other people and much later. I believe that I inherited too much kindness from my parents, which can be a bad trait sometimes. Even if someone hurts me, I can easily forget about it. I feel that this form of kindness of the heart makes one vulnerable for exploitation.

My paternal grandfather was the only doctor in Daraa, and thus the main destination for many people. People I met in town always have a nice story about him. He was poor even though he was treating countless people. He just had a piece of land which he gave away. My aunt once told me that he used to fill tote bags with wheat, and at night he would go around to the houses of people in need and leave the bags in front of the doors.

When we were growing up, I wasn't aware of any sectarian differences within Islam. I knew that we were Sunnis, but I didn't know about other minorities. My father used to drive us to the Alawite Mountains near Latakia every summer. We lived all together harmoniously as Syrians. We used to celebrate Christian holidays with our Christian neighbors even though the province of Daraa is very conservative. We have very strict traditions and customs unlike other provinces. But you see, if you raise your children in certain ways you can still give them some space. We lived close to my maternal grandparents, and sometimes my grandfather wouldn't even have his breakfast without us.

Ah, let me tell you about our typical breakfast. We would have flat bread, eggs, zaatar with delicious olive oil. Daraa is famous for its olive oil. We maintained our olive groves and raised our own wheat. The breakfast would also include homemade Labni/Labneh, which we preserved in olive oil so it wouldn't go bad.

Cross-Generational Negotiations Against the Ayıp List

The notion of *ayıp* (inappropriate behavior) is very important in our society. I learned what was considered *ayıp* early on and I passed it to my children, so they would display respectful manners, dress properly, etcetera. *Ayıp* is such a large umbrella term that the list of *ayıps* [*plural*] is too long to cite here. What might be *ayıp* for us may not be *ayıp* in other cultures or even families, but I would say that there is a collective agreement about certain sets of moral rules in Syria. One example is that women should not laugh out loud in public, so when my fourteen-year-old daughter does that, I have to warn and keep her quiet on the street. However, I must add that she is still a child inside; it is only her body that developed quickly so she looks older than her age. She acts indifferent and sometimes rebellious; it is not always easy to convince her about our *ayıp* list.

My earliest memory regarding school is getting into trouble with a girl who broke my arm and ripped my clothes after a major fight in the school yard. My father was called, and he took me to the hospital to get my arm cast. I remember crying hard and announcing him that I no longer wanted to go to school. He told me very calmly that she was just a little girl, and everything was going to be okay. I also remember my general excitement with starting primary school, especially the first few weeks of the school year.

My mother didn't allow us to mix with other students, which meant returning home immediately after school except to visit our relatives. I wished she would allow us to attend a birthday party even just once. We were four girls, which is why my mother was very protective about our family name. I am practicing the same rules now with my teenage daughter. She doesn't have friends here in Istanbul, but once she mentioned a birthday party. When I asked her if she would like to go, she said no, probably anticipating my reply in case she wanted to attend.

I acknowledge my need for constant validation since I feel that I sometimes lack balance and confidence, especially regarding my principles and values in life. I have always been a timid person with fears. I am not sure why it was and is still the case, but I guess it might be because of my mother who constantly reproached and criticized me for my actions. In contrast to the fears I had, there was also an unquenchable curiosity in me to the point that

I would break things apart and try to fix them again. I would attempt to cook the most difficult local dishes such as *kibbeh* to test my cooking skills when my mom wasn't home, making a big mess in the kitchen.

When I was at the two-year vocational institute, learning handicrafts, sewing, and embroidering, I was also very dedicated to the assignments. I once slept on my work while trying to finish a table cover. It is my personality. With the trouble I caused to my parents, sometimes I wished my father had beaten me, but he never did. I think there are times when strict discipline and penalizing children is needed.[1]

The Roots of Some Old and New Fears as a Woman

I want to get along with and be accepted by my community, which I kind of lost in Turkey. I am grateful to have a good Syrian neighbor named Assaliya whom I can visit and share my problems with, but I don't feel welcomed to or part of the Turkish culture yet. Without other people around me, life is not as nice. I value establishing good relations with my neighbors and mixing up with other families. When Assaliya doesn't visit us every other day, I feel depressed and out of my mind. I love having people around. We are in a major transition period as Syrians, and we don't know where to unite as a family again. There is something new every day, some of which requires adjustment on our part. Not knowing Turkish is a major hurdle in getting around and making friends.

There are times when I feel helpless. Being away from my two children is very difficult. We fled Syria with our lives, and we are now living as refugees, so I don't see the point of making life more difficult in one's own house. Before the migration, my husband was always very jealous of other men. Even in my mid-thirties, I couldn't even crack a window freely. He also used to argue that a woman shouldn't be given "sweet talk" because she would get spoiled and change her attitude. Now that is gone, and he even encourages me to register in language courses. Still, he has his crazy moments that are triggered by the nagging of his parents and sister. He has no reason to be jealous of me because I inform him of any unusual manner displayed by a man. Once I received an anonymous phone call by a man who told me that it was a sin and mistake to be married to "this useless husband of yours." Maybe some women would have chosen to hide such an unpleasant thing from their husbands, but I didn't. I tell Ahmad everything as a precaution, because men can arrange things on purpose to test their women.

In high school, I didn't have any crushes or anyone in particular who stood out. I liked boys' attention, but I never responded. I feared men. I was not bold enough to do anything like that. I asked myself then and today, and I ask you, girls might wish for a relationship especially when they see friends dating, but when you think about it, do these relationships actually work? I don't think they last long. There is no such thing as love, right? Everyone has different convictions, and this is mine.

I used to have very soft skin and rosy cheeks. My hair was long, and sometimes my mother braided it. In high school, we had a national security instructor who liked punishing me for no reason. She would make me crawl on my knees and elbows around the school courtyard. I think she was jealous of me. One of the most important life lessons is not to trust female friends. I believe there is always jealousy and envy among girlfriends so one needs to be careful. Because I personally had to go through such experiences many times, I taught this lesson to my daughters too.

A week ago [*mid–April 2016*], I was sitting with my husband by the sea-side. I was lost in thought and he asked me what I was thinking of. I made a statement about the negative effects of his family in our life, and he acknowledged it for the first time after all these years. I think he has begun to understand what was going on and how badly I have been hurt. I hope he keeps this awakening.

Pushing Around, Pushing Back: Marriage and Children

Maybe I should talk about how I met my husband Ahmad. I was almost seventeen, although I never felt like a teenager. Meeting boys and talking about them were the most popular activities among girls. I used to dance, dress up, strengthen my long hair, and wear makeup, all inside the house of course. My mother would reproach me for doing these things but putting on makeup made me feel like an adult.

I fenced off the boys who would ask me out because I was convinced by my father's view and didn't want to do anything behind his back. These "friendship requests" were a bit of trouble during my high school years. The most significant memory regarding my youth was the marriage proposals that my father rejected consistently on the excuse of us getting higher education first. Ironically, my husband isn't educated.

After high school, I began attending a vocational institute for women. One day, I noticed that Ahmad was following me, but I didn't pay any attention. In fact, I never saw him until he proposed. I had several marriage proposals at the time. He also sent his sister to ask for my hand, but my father rejected it because Ahmad was not educated and I didn't know him.

However, Ahmad didn't give up, and he tried with other middle-people until my dad finally agreed to receive him. I didn't want to meet him, and my mother supported me. I reminded my father about our minimum criterion of having a university diploma when it came to his future son-in-law. In return, he told me that there are other things too but couldn't provide us a sound argument. I remember one thing that made my father very upset. Ahmad and a relative of my father who also proposed at around the same time started a fight over who was going to marry me at a gas station and made quite a scene. Someone called my father and told him about this incident, which must have been very embarrassing for him to hear.

In the end, my father kind of forced me into this marriage probably because he was getting very tired of Ahmad's insistence, the people he kept sending to my father with the same intention, and the gossip around all these. The only option that was left to me was to make impossible demands regarding my dowry to frustrate Ahmad and his family, but that didn't work either. There are many small anecdotes about my strategy, but they all failed.[2]

We were engaged for about eight months. During our engagement, whenever he wanted to touch me or hold my hand, I would scream. Once he came to our house to visit me, and I was applying nail polish on my fingernails. By that time, my mother began to like him, so she invited him in and left us alone in the room. He asked me if he could apply the polish on my nails, and I refused but he insisted. I finally allowed him and as he was applying it he suddenly kissed me, and I went mad. I yelled at him and he went out of the room to tell my mother that he kissed me because he wanted to. I cried all night and I made him promise not to do such sudden things again. I was eighteen and he was twenty-seven.

Gradually, I came to the conclusion that he loved me so much, and I began to feel love toward him too. When you meet someone who wants you that strongly, you should love him back. Yes, that's what happened. After a while, I felt that my soul belonged to him. It is the other people, his family in particular, who have affected his attitude toward me. When he bought me a ring, he asked me not to wear it in his family's presence. He would never show affection or say nice words to me unless when we are alone.

Marrying Ahmad was the most significant decision of my life. It helped me to come to conclusions on love and marriage. As a teenager, I used to read some self-help books for the prospective brides, and to be honest, I was never convinced by them. I met women and men who were so much in love but after they got married they went through hell. Love may grow in time, so it is possible to get married without falling in love as long as the essential qualities of the couple are compatible such as submission to God, having a good heart, and mutual respect. My husband sometimes changed my life for the better and improved it, sometimes for the worse. We have four children, three daughters and a son. They are my biggest accomplishments in life. I hope that I will never forget any details about my children.

My son Mohamed and I have similar characters, kind but quick-tempered. He always prays on time. His success in high school was very important for me because my husband's side of the family was waiting for his failure. Most of them can't pass beyond high school so I am glad my children are making progress. His dad bought Mohamed a car as a graduation gift, which was nice. Mohamed then completed the first year of Economics with distinction in Syria. However, once the government started arresting young men, I made him leave for Jordan. He finished a two-year-pharmacology institute there and found a job right after graduation. He was working almost ten hours a day, but the Jordanian laws banned Syrians from work. He also attended English courses because his goal is to live in the U.S., so I sold my last gold bracelets for financing his plans. They were my father's gift, and I was keeping them for any emergency surgery. He got accepted by a university in the U.S., paid the registration fee, but the U.S. Embassy rejected his student visa application four times.

My oldest daughter is in Syria with her husband and their new-born baby. She knows what I have been going through. If something happens to me, she will be the mother to her sisters. Regardless of the physical distance, she can make me feel like I am with her. My middle daughter is fourteen years old. She can act indifferently toward people around her. She rebels against her father's attitudes and encourages me to leave him. I tell her that life is not as simple, and one needs to learn to be patient, but she doesn't listen to me. My youngest is four years old. She is a cutie, and completely clueless about life.

My in-laws caused me a lot of suffering, which began from the very first weeks of my engagement. They have never forgotten the days when I demanded unreasonable things to put off the marriage, and they made sure that I paid for them. Because of their egging him on, my husband divorced me once.

I will never forget the day and I still have no idea what caused the whole incident. After work, my husband stopped by his parents' house on the first floor; then, he came up to our house, which was on the second floor of the same building. He told me to leave the house or else he'd divorce me. I was confused and asked what had happened, he didn't tell me anything but repeated his order. When I refused to leave, he told me "I divorce you now" and then I had to leave. My son joined me and shouted at his grandfather, "Are you happy now, is that what you wanted? They're divorced now!" My father-in-law followed us and even beat my son with his walking stick. I stopped my son to respond in anger although his arms were scratched, and his grandfather was still cursing us behind our back.

It would be too embarrassing to show up like this at my parents' house, so I told my son to go to them and asked for some money on my behalf. I decided to visit my husband's uncle, the only reasonable person I could think of, so that he can be the arbitrator in this shocking event. We spent two nights at their house during which his uncle tried to convince my husband and in-laws, but they didn't want me back.[3]

I had to go to my parents' house and spend three depressing months. I was even hospitalized due to a bleeding problem and stayed two days at the hospital. I was pregnant with our third child. I wanted people to leave me alone with my children. I wished my mother were with me at the hospital but according to our traditions, she couldn't. The incident happened soon after my father's passing so she wasn't supposed to leave the house for three months as a widow.

Although I treated my husband's family very kindly, only his uncle agreed to be the mediator, and thus we resumed the marriage after three months. The smallest gestures make us bigger humans. Living with my in-laws in Turkey is even more challenging since I have no place to go when they throw me out of the house. My husband and I had had such a good time in Istanbul before they joined us. However, our story of leaving Syria is not very pleasant.

One night, my husband's friend came to our house and told Ahmad that his name was on the military recruitment list, so he had to leave the country immediately. We left three days after this news, although I felt sick and was suspicious of getting breast cancer. My husband didn't listen to me. He simply booked our flights, and we flew to Istanbul. The girls joined us, the eldest has her own family so she chose to stay in Syria.

Merging Yet Conflicting: On Islam and Traditions

I grew up in a very conservative environment. Unlike Damascus, Daraa has a tribal system. Men sit around to see what girls are up to and gossip about other people's daughters without considering their own. When extra-marital relations happen, people won't speak about them, but some would even kill their daughters if they are involved in such affairs. My father told us about these stories. Here in Istanbul, people mind their own business, which I prefer.

I was so lucky to have a progressive father who knew how to communicate and reason with his children. I remember how my mother announced once that riding bicycles for girls was *ayıp*, but my father brought me one despite her objections. He just didn't pay any attention to her or the neighbors. I felt lucky and nurtured as a child.

Our religion is a religion of goodness, and it is easy to follow. My interpretation is that the religion shouldn't make your life difficult. However, our ideas differ within the family. For example, I don't think celebrating my children's birthdays is against Islam, but my husband says, "It's haram, we don't have this kind of celebration in our religion." Our four-year-old daughter begged me to have a birthday party, to which my husband responded, "There's no need for that; it's wrong." I got her a present and told that it's from both parents, so I included my husband in it.

These haram-halal issues in Islam are hard to explain to small children. I found it very challenging to convince my daughters that celebrating the Mother's Day is practiced only for the women in my husband's family and not for their own mother. Consequently, I get a grumpy face from the teenager, while my four-year-old Faryal poses the innocent question, "Mommy, why are we celebrating the Mother's Day of the grandma but not my birthday?" At least Zaynab responds positively to me when I tell her to dress in long skirts.

There are traditions that are passed from one generation to another, but a person needs to be wise to see and explain the logic behind them. For instance, my son wanted to smoke a waterpipe (*narghile*) in his senior year in high school. My husband said, "I will kill him if I see him smoke." I tried to reason with him saying that it was only a phase that our son was going through. I brought *narghile* to the house and smoked with him. I heard some bad stories about youngsters putting marijuana or other drugs into waterpipes and becoming addicts. When a parent is wise, he or she should allow the space of liberty to their children and let them try things, similar to what my father did one generation ago.

One way to keep traditions intact is to have good communication with your children. My son lives in Jordan (as of 2017). I call him every day and ask him to contact his father and get his advice about things. My oldest daughter in Syria is raising her one-and-a-half-year-old baby, so I talk to her every day and listen to the accounts of her daily life. She consults me even with the kind of food that she prepares for the day. People compliment my cooking, but I learned it all from my mother, which is part of passing traditions. When it comes to instilling religious practices, once again, parents play an important role. Like this morning, I woke my daughter up for the prayer. She doesn't pray often, but I still do my best to remind and sometimes ask her to join me. I can't force her though.

I wish I were in Syria to enjoy being a grandmother and helping my oldest daughter in person. But the winds of life always blow as they wish, and we are powerless against them. Not all women are submissive though. I have to mention here my paternal aunt who was very respected in Daraa. I used to look up to her, but I can never be like her. She resolved disputes among women in her community or finalized engagements for future couples, etcetera. My other paternal aunts were also very open-minded and bold, but here I am, still shy and cowardly, I fear. If things are considered *ayıp*, I would stay away from them regardless of my personal opinion.

Grappling with Wounded Hopes and Bodies

On March 18, 2011, I was at home, shortly after the Jumaa (Friday) prayer. The protests began with people's chanting, "God, Syria, Freedom!" My house was on the third floor of the apartment building. We went up to the fourth floor to watch, and it looked beautiful. The streets were full of people as far as eyes could see, and they were chanting slogans of freedom and dismantling the regime, all combined with *Allahu Akbar* (God is Great). It would give goosebumps to any eyewitness. Sometimes I think it was good that people came out; then I change my mind and wish that people hadn't taken to the streets. Looking at how things have turned out, I get burdened with doubts.

During the revolution, I got connected to the Red Crescent and mobilized the women in my neighborhood. The soldiers who were fighting for the regime broke into the vicinity and tried to arrest as many young men as possible, so we hid them. They used teargas extensively and as a result, many demonstrators fell unconscious. We were prepared to treat them with water, Coke, and onion. As soon as we saw a young man falling on the ground, we ran to him, washed his face with Coke, and it worked. We also dragged injured people inside to tend their wounds, and we carried dead bodies into our houses to practice pre-burial rituals. I was five months pregnant then, my husband wasn't around, and I had to hide my own son.

There are a few instances that are engraved in my mind, which will be very hard to forget. One officer on the street hit a young demonstrator with the back of his gun. I ran to the officer and told him that the young man was my son. He already fell unconscious, so I took him from the officer's hands, washed his face, and put on a bandage. Afterward, he was transferred to the field hospital. For the rest of the world, this may be the expected order that the injured needs to follow. However, in Syria, things are different. If someone enters the hospital as wounded, his body disappears, and nobody knows where to claim it. If he was alive when he was accepted at the hospital, it no longer shocks me to learn that he died there. The state hospitals are not reliable centers of ethical treatment in Syria; they are sites of murder.

My second memory relates to my friend's son, her only child. I saw the police shooting him in the head. We immediately carried him to a house, but he had already passed away. It was very painful both to witness a young man die right in plain sight and to have her mother, your friend, screaming, almost losing her mind. The last incident happened in my neighborhood, very close to my house. There was a mother with six daughters, who left home because they were afraid to be bombed. As they were running to the mosque as a safe shelter, a mortar fell on them. There was no hospital or ambulance nearby. We put their bodies in a truck and brought them in a warehouse cooler which was used to keep the yogurt supply for the whole neighborhood. Who knows when was the last time that the giant fridge harbored yogurt in it instead of preserving raw human flesh?

The lack of basic treatment materials such as disinfection solutions and bandage claimed too many lives. When these seven women's lives were lost after the bombardment, we still had to continue our tasks to provide ice, water, disinfectants, and bandages to every household. We constantly risked our lives, but we had to do it regardless of the time of the day. We worked at midnights too when it was pitch dark since the government cut electricity along with water and all communications. We all knew that there were snipers on the top of the buildings around. It was either them or the mortars that could have killed us any time. Seven lives withered right in front of my eyes, and I still wonder today how I was able to continue running around and distributing the limited supply of medical equipment half-blindly to the young men hidden here and there. I must have followed their voices rather than their moves because it was too dark to see anything.

Dreams and Ambitions

I wanted to become a flight attendant but when I shared my dream with my father, he disagreed. He encouraged me to study medicine or engineering instead, to which I replied, "But that's what everyone does. I want to be different." Now my younger daughter's dream is to be an aviation engineer although I tell her that it is difficult for girls. She sounds determined but you know how teenagers are like, they change their minds too often. We'll see what is written in her destiny.

I may have failed to achieve my dreams, but I hope my children will be successful and make theirs come true. Sometimes Mohamed plays with the idea of going to Germany but then changes his mind due to the challenges of learning a new language and starting all over again. I have to encourage him even though imagining him all by himself in Germany scares and kills me internally [*Lutfia cries*].

Reaching my forties was not joyful because of the feeling that many years had already passed, and I haven't achieved much regarding what I wanted to do in this life. You close one eyelid, open the other, and time flies. I don't like disappointments because I can't handle them well. I feel that I am about to explode and die, which ends in crying a lot. In difficult times, there are two men I consult to: My son Mohamed and my younger brother in Canada whose name is also Mohamed. My brother recently reminded me of a Bedouin proverb "You can still take your revenge after forty years," and told me to be patient. I said to him that I didn't want revenge or get back at anyone; it wasn't the proper advice for me on this specific issue with my in-laws. I just wanted my brother to know what I was going through in Istanbul.

I could have never imagined having my house bombed and beginning a life from scratch in a new country whose language I cannot speak. I was hoping to marry off my son and help him open a business in Syria, but now our everything is gone, and we have to start all over again. I remember as a teenager, when my father took me to Homs and another time, my mother took me to Damascus only for a few days, but I missed home and wanted to return. I have always been that type of a person.

When you are optimistic or have a partner that incites optimism, then you can feel like twenty again and be full of energy, but when your spouse puts you down … [*pause*]. The truth is I don't want to get old. My spirit is young and will remain young. Look, I am wearing jeans [*under her baggy coat*]. I enjoy learning new things and I am one of the oldest students in my Turkish and computer classes, but I don't mind. When I feel depressed, which happens when I am at home here, I go out to walk. Do you know what my favorite thing is? Putting on my boots and walking outside by myself! It is not right to be a pessimist and my mood gets better as soon as I leave the house.

Working as a teacher after finishing vocational school was really nice. My father found the job for me. He wanted me to be out of that house and its problems, and to do something useful with my time, so he asked me if I wanted to teach. Then, he talked to my husband who agreed. I tutored at *al*

Ghouta, a school that was run by UNICEF. If I had continued working and got an early retirement, I would have been paid in dollars, and I wouldn't have needed assistance from anybody. My husband regrets a lot for making me quit my job to satisfy others' whims [*she means the in-laws*]. Contributing to one's community can be practiced in various forms. Teaching was one of them and I truly enjoyed it.

Feeling independent and experiencing an active life outside home also made me love *al Ghouta* school. Now in Istanbul, I can't wait until I visit the NGO in Esenler. If I stayed at home, I would be arguing and facing problems with my mother-in-law. I feel suffocated if I don't leave the house. This week I was so tired because my husband's overweight mother wanted to go for an outing. My neck and back hurt badly from pushing her in her wheelchair up and down the hills of Istanbul. Why does it have to be me, not her own son or daughter? The same thing is true for groceries. It's all on me. She creates such a drama whenever her blood pressure gets high too, and I have to endure the worst of insults and caprices.

In addition to the in-law and marital issues, I also suffer from health problems, so things are not getting any better, but I still feel gratitude toward Allah. I went to a public hospital here in Istanbul, but the doctor didn't properly examine me. She just asked about my blood pressure and after ten days I went back with the test results. She checked my blood pressure and repeated that I should come back in ten days. Life is difficult here when one doesn't know where to go or who to talk with. Recently, I asked my aunt to send me a few boxes of diabetes medicine from United Arab Emirates, where it is relatively inexpensive. God bless her soul, the medicine arrived with additional cold and flu medications. I am leaving my health now up to God. I am learning Turkish so maybe my daily life gets easier.

A friend of mine told me about an NGO where Syrians can get assistance in Istanbul. Initially, I felt sorry for myself because asking for help was not easy, but I went ahead. I met several women there and even gave a talk on Syrian children's education at a panel in March 2016, which made me feel like an important person. The same positive feelings arose with this life history project. I realized that there are some people who cared, who bothered to listen, and understood me [*Lutfia cries*].

Spirituality Rooted in the Quran

The term "spirituality" is somewhat unclear to me, so I am not sure if my response is satisfactory. I sometimes wonder how I got here or why I am here. In Syria, I used to have a garden which I enjoyed tending to and it would tend to my soul in return. Whenever I watered the plants and sat down with a cup of coffee in my hand, I used to feel as if I transcended of this world. Is it spirituality?

Here, in Istanbul, when I sit by the coast and watch the sea and seagulls, I forget all about this life and its issues. However, there is always something pulling me out of it, several responsibilities are waiting for me. I don't know how to expand on these moments further; maybe it is better not to answer.

When I pray, I feel that God answers my prayers. I sense that I'm being heard. Maybe God bestowed this gift upon me. I don't know, maybe because I have a kind heart and God responds to that. I love all people, wish the best for them, and God never disappoints me *Alhamdulillah* (all praise is due to God alone). This is a special feeling like no other. God creates and manages everything for us. It's all in his hands. "No misfortune can happen, either in the earth or in yourselves, that was not set down in writing before We brought it into being" (Quran: 57: 22).

My inner strength comes from God, and my concern of raising two young daughters also provides me the potency to continue with my life rather than simply collapse. Thank Allah that I am more knowledgeable about Islam now than in my twenties, and reading the Quran is my main guidance and consolation. When I feel down, I seek refuge in the verses of the Quran. I hope I will never forget praying or the Quranic verses since they are the most valuable for me. Life is also full of gifts, both benevolent and bad; personal experiences in life are part of the package as well. Some days, the best gifts are words which are spoken with kindness and appreciation. Serving someone without receiving a single word of appreciation is very disappointing.

Whenever so much tension builds up at home and we are about to burst, I listen to the Quran and feel that God calms down the whole house and grants me some peace. Most importantly, I place the fear of God before my eyes to maintain peace in me. After coming to Turkey, I feel that I have become more religious. It is subtle, but I can sense it even when the others around me don't.

The secret to maintaining peace in one's self is loving everyone, wishing them well, and pray God that they find the straight path to Allah, even when they treat you badly. It's best for your own soul not to harbor any hate in you. I am very pleased to have talked about my life and many issues. I opened up and dug up the well in me by talking to you. I feel happy about this experience.

The Author's Touch

On March 16, 2016, a Saturday afternoon, I attended a public event entitled "Being a Refugee Woman in Turkey." I was introduced to Lutfia, one of the panelists, after the talk by the Community Outreach Assistant of the NGO which organized the panel.[4] Lutfia warmly returned my appreciative words on her agreement to share her life story with me. I promised to arrange an interpreter as soon as possible in order to begin the interviews.

One of my favorite lines in Lutfia's accounts is, "As long as someone is living, he/she is learning something because new things will come up all the time." Lutfia underlines that people learn only from their own experiences and not from others,' something which I have reservations about. In the given context, however, she arrived at this conclusion in order to justify the course of events since she got married and had to survive the post–2011 conflict era as well as her family problems.

As of April 2018, Lutfia continues to live in Istanbul with her family and is active in the educational work regarding Syrian children through the NGO staff who introduced us two years ago.

3

Muzna's Story

The Cloud That Harbors Heavy Showers

June 2016: After a long day at work, Muzna arrived in Gezi Patisserie in Taksim, Istanbul. It is an old and elegant café whose name became world-famous due to the Gezi Park Protests in 2013. I ordered coffee and she asked for a cold glass of lemonade. Muzna's energy is contagious and inspiring. She calls herself a feminist and insists on using her real name in the book. During the interview, she referred to her smart phone many times for checking out some vocabulary, showing me pictures, or websites. She apologized for her English and wished that the interview was in French.

As soon as Muzna got back home, she sent me three attachments by email, one article and two reports: Cynthia Cockburn's "Exit from War: Syrian Women Learn from the Bosnian Women's Movement" in which Muzna is featured by name and picture, the 58th CEDAW Session Report, and "Seeking Accountability and Effective Response for Gender-Based Violence Against Syrian Women" by MADRE. She keeps in touch since then, sometimes inter-mittently, and this chapter presents selected scenes and fragments of her active virtual presence across the world.

My mind makes constant connections between the trees that are being uprooted, cut down or "relocated" to some places designated by the author-ities and my Turkish and Syrian friends whose creative minds are restricted by visa requirements. Their bodies are controlled by the ones whose main duty is to constrain and suspect people. The fact that refugees are uprooted and resettled by some people in power ranging from traffickers to presidents brings them closer to the beautiful trees that I have in mind, including the ones at Gezi Park.

I asked Muzna what her name meant in Arabic since I have learned dur-ing my interviews that most names in Syria have meanings like we do in

Turkey. "The cloud which harbors heavy showers," was her answer. I wonder if she believes in the power of one's first name and the destiny it might bring to its carrier.

The Family Ties and the Seeds of Revolution

I was born at a military hospital in Damascus on January 20, 1991. It was the end of the First Gulf War. My mother said that nobody was around when she gave birth to me because the staff were busy with more serious cases than worrying about new babies [she laughs].

We lived in a religious but not extremist neighborhood. I have two brothers. The older one studied Chemistry at the University of Granada in Spain, and he plans to live there and work at the labs. We are very close and share the same political ideas. We communicate everyday by WhatsApp. My younger brother is in the emergency medical services program at King Saud University in Riyadh. Initially, he was enrolled at the therapy medicine program; however, he switched after one year to the emergency services because of the way that the war affected him.

One thing I inherited from my parents is their commitment to the idea of Revolution. Please capitalize the R in the word. We all were raised by hearing constantly that we needed to be honest individuals, always prioritizing the community needs over our personal ones so that the struggle for a better society can continue even if I am tired and feel that all my energy is gone.

My parents have been very active in the Revolution. My mother is in the humanitarian aid area and my father does extra work in translation from Russian to Arabic and the other way around. He was trained as an academic in European languages and his fulltime teaching job is the reason why we ended up in Riyadh. Something that I have carried over from Syrian culture is to be friendly, which may not necessarily be a Syrian value, but I believe it is.

My earliest memory is attending primary school for the first time, accompanied by my parents. My childhood was so much fun. We practiced sports, it was like a summer camp all the time. I took violin lessons with my father's encouragement. I have many nice memories but now our life has become very complicated. As for my teenage years, I remember reading a lot, I was a real bookworm. Other than that, nothing really stands out.

I grew up as a vegetarian and I was very conscious about it. Only recently I was forced to eat some meat because according to the doctor, avoiding meat was the reason for my constant fatigue and caused low iron and hemoglobin level in my blood. I don't know but meat is not easy to consume. Among my favorite foods are *tabbuleh, fattoush,* and *zaatar,* and I also drink a lot of tea like Turkish people. I love *molehiya* but without meat.

I owe my energy to my commitment to freedom and Revolution. I am convinced that most Syrians are against the Assad regime even if they can't express it. I know that they hope to replace it one day with a new political system that respects the rights of Syrians, including the right to hold their elected officials accountable. I will do my best to contribute to this wherever I am, and I feel that I have nothing to lose now. Most of my old friends in Syria stopped talking to me or having anything to do with me because of my activism and political views. Their abandonment made me a new being, I have a completely different circle of friends now.

I am a very honest and very hard-working person. I am also shy, well, I used to describe myself as simply "shy" which always surprised people until I got to Canada. Here, I was given a long personality test before the selection of Montreal's Young Leaders' Team. The results which were made up of 30-page long analysis of my perceptions, personality, how I make decisions and so forth, concluded that I was an introvert, a different and fancier term than just shy. I finally understood why I never liked talking much. I need to get better as a public speaker. I am still working on this without feeling bad about being an introvert.

I have more freedom and time to be an activist and being single helps me to organize my life as I want. My family have supported me in all my decisions. However privileged this might sound, I am still the victim of what has been happening in Syria; yet, the constant feeling of guilt has never left me.

Your question on my role models is a challenging one. However, since I just mentioned the advantages of being single when it comes to taking bolder steps in certain situations, I immediately thought of Rania Abbasi. She was a dentist, social activist, and national chess champion of Syria. She was detained by the government agents on March 11, 2013, along with her husband and six children in Damascus. I can't imagine how horribly Rania must have suffered in a state prison somewhere in Syria with her family. I usually find myself asking whether my participation in the Revolution would have been the same if I had children. I think keeping yourself fearless when you have small children like Rania is a real challenge. As of 2018, she and her family are listed among the disappeared since the Syrian government denied any information. I can only hope maybe they managed to escape and are in hiding.

Secondly, Razan Zaitouneh, who is one of the most powerful women that I have ever known, is among my role models. She is a Syrian human rights lawyer, civil society activist, and the co-founder of the Violations Documentation Centre in Syria. She was deeply involved in the Syrian Revolution. In December 2013, Zaitouneh was kidnapped along with her husband, Wael Hamadeh, and two colleagues, Samira Khalil and Nazem Hammadi, in the opposition-held town of Douma to the north of Damascus. As of March 2018, their whereabouts were still unknown. It is suspected that the Islamist Salafi rebel group Army of Islam was responsible. I posted her photograph as my profile picture on Facebook.

I can't think of any other role models at the moment except my parents. It is mainly because I believe in ideas more than the people so my focus stays on thoughts and I fail remembering names or faces. Let's say that I meet someone and may admire her academic achievements. Then, I observe and appreciate another person's interpretations of Islam. Later on, I meet someone else and am impressed by his generosity, this goes on and on.

All these people have unique qualities and when I add them up, there comes an ideal person who doesn't exist. I admire anyone who can maintain her honesty and stick to her inner ethics even when there is a war going on outside, where rules or laws are no longer valid. I can't name particular books or movies which have influenced me, either. I read many books and see a lot of movies. However, there is one book called *Quiet: The Power of Introverts in a World That Can't Stop Talking* by Susan Cain, which I recently read and felt relieved by some of the ideas and research results there. I also read that the Turkish author Elif Shafak is an introvert, too, so I am happy to share this trait with her!

Relationships and Partners

I met him during an anti-government gathering and we took part at the demonstrations. In 2014, we got married but only performed the religious ceremony. The Syrian government refused to register us because they didn't (still don't) want activists to get any official papers. Nevertheless, we managed to leave for France together since we wanted to continue our studies there. However, he began changing in attitude and behavior in front of my eyes and became a person who was acting like a traditional Middle Eastern macho. He intervened in my work and acted aggressively too. I still have no clue why marriage changed him so radically.

Our unregistered marriage lasted five months after which I left for Saudi Arabia and stayed with my parents for three months to recover. This relationship affected me negatively. In fact, it was the first time I experienced depression because I blamed myself for failing to see what was coming. As a women's rights defender, it was most ironical. I was already helping others to reclaim their rights and freedom as women and I almost lost them in my own private space.

You jokingly commented that you wouldn't want to be my partner because I would have no time for him or us as a couple, but I disagree. If he is committed to the same cause, that relationship can evolve beautifully. My parents are a good example. We can all be sitting at a different corner of the living room with our gadgets and be connected to many different people electronically. However, we are serving to the same cause and working for the true liberation of Syria with a similar mindset. You can hear my parents' reading out, commenting, sharing one case or story, swearing at the computer screen, but they are collaborating with each other as well. That's how I see it and I'd like to practice it with my future partner too.

In comparison to the other women of my age in my circle, my life and personality have been very different. All my female cousins assumed traditional roles by which I mean getting married right after secondary school or university and having three or four children. They are practicing Muslims and wear headscarves in public, and they wouldn't dare to have premarital sex. However, let me open a parenthesis here since most of these seemingly traditional Syrian women went through major changes with the Revolution especially if they had to be displaced. Clearly, displacement wasn't by choice, but I am glad that some of them gained independency in exile because they were separated from their husbands and no longer expected to fulfill their gender roles in Syria. I know many women who began to work abroad, make a living, traveled alone across several borders, study, and have boyfriends in exile, which would be disapproved or punishable depending on where they lived in Syria.

Premarital relationships between men and women are not accepted publicly in Syria so we all had them secretly. The problem is not just our society but also the Syrian government itself which claims to be secular. However, there has always been a "vice squad" or "morality police" as the direct translation goes. They can go into the house of a couple who live together without a marriage contract and arrest them based on a law which punishes people for transgressing and dishonoring the institution of marriage or something like that. I can't find the exact words to translate this law, and even if I could, it would not make much sense to the readers in the West, right? I leave it up to their imagination to figure out the fate of same-sex couples if they are detained. In Canada, the refugees must attend sessions about human rights and there is sex education in public schools. Currently they come as a culture shock for most newcomers, but these open talks about sexual and reproductive health as well as same-sex couples' human rights will be very good for the second generation.

I came to Istanbul for a conference in 2015 which was organized by a Swiss NGO and I fell in love with the city. I feel at home here. I told my parents that Istanbul is where I wanted to live and work so we rented a flat and I found an NGO position at Badael ("Alternatives" in English). Badael was founded for strengthening Syrian NGOs and promoting non-violence, and since then I have been conducting mostly online training for Syrian women in Syria and Turkey. I also spent one year in Gaziantep, but that was before the marriage episode. I made more friends in Gaziantep than in Istanbul. The reason is simple: Istanbul is a big city and people have no time for each other; Gaziantep is more provincial and informal.

My future partner needs to accept me as I am, that is, I will work non-stop for my community and might decline his invitations to fancy restaurants. If he wants me to fulfill the traditional roles of a housewife, I am sorry, it's not going to happen. I don't plan on baking a cake when I can fix the daily problems of Syrian women who are in need, even from a distance. Regrettably, I have developed a fear of men's changing their attitudes and not showing their real faces after my bad experience. However, what I went through is not unique. To be with a feminist activist can pose a big problem for majority of men, I suspect. That is the main reason for my stress on gender revolution whenever I refer to the Revolution. They can't be considered separately.

Being a Syrian in Turkey

Turkish people are very friendly, I feel at home in general. In the neighborhood where I am living [*Şişli, June 2016*], there is no discrimination against Syrians, but in some other areas, I also hear some bad stories from time to time like you do. I am often asked where I am from, while shopping for example. Most Turkish people respond back, "But you don't look Syrian."

Most Syrians see Turkey as a place of transition so they don't bother learning the language or the culture. They ought to acknowledge the possibility that this so-called temporary period can last up to two or three years if not longer. This psychology can be very difficult to deal with for Syrians and it may lead to discriminatory acts on the other end, and I can understand them.

My own friends are reluctant to learn Turkish because they call Turkey their "transitional locale." Learning the language can ease the adaptation and save you from many unpleasant situations. You can read the public signs and warnings. I can make the list of advantages longer, especially for Syrian women.

We need to create an awareness together with Turkish peace activists about the Syrians' presence. Not all Syrians are here to take the Turks' jobs. Plus, our status as "guests" is very vulnerable in Turkey. For sake of protection and knowing one's rights, I prefer to be granted a refugee status instead of being a "guest" although the latter sounds nicer. I hope in near future, the Turkish government can regulate its laws on this growing problem because we cannot fully function without a status, especially as peace activists or as NGO workers in general. We usually work in disguise and get registered under Turkish people's names which can cause several problems. All Syrians' future and status in Turkey are ambiguous, which causes extra stress for any displaced individual.

My Life and Work After March 2011

When the demonstrations began in Syria in March 2011, I was a twenty-year-old student of French language and linguistics. My human rights activism started on Facebook and then we took to the streets of Damascus. My uncles and cousins were abused and beaten during the demonstrations. I learned about my own uncle's detention through an anonymously posted report on FB. I then contacted some representatives of Human Rights Watch via Skype and shared the evidence. I had many relatives and friends who got detained, injured, or killed so I decided to leave the country and continue my struggle for freedom and human dignity from Turkey.

I traveled to Lebanon and Jordan while in Turkey, visited several refugee camps, helped organizing humanitarian aid distribution before I decided to focus on all forms of violence against women. I chose this particular area because of a text message that I found in my phone, which basically said something like, "If you want to get married, choose a Syrian, they are beautiful and cheap." I got so furious and decided to do something against it.

I made a quick search and found out that there were several middle-women who arrange these so-called marriages or trafficking. I also observed that many parents in the camps or city borders "sold" their daughters in the disguise of marriage for money and protection. They were not getting the basic aid from the government or international agencies for a variety of reasons so marrying off their daughters to mostly old men was the only option for their survival. By the way, as for young boys, they were being recruited to fight and become soldiers.

I prepared fliers with basic information and used a simple language for the parents at the refugee camps, "If you want to marry off your daughters, make sure to register them in the government records. They are not for sale, we want to help your daughters. If you don't want the marriage in future, you can give us a call." There was a hotline number and also a FB link on the flier.

Unlike Turkey, getting access to the refugee camps in Jordan and Lebanon was easy. I had friends who worked at some NGOs there, and I would join them. To learn the number of forced marriages in the camps, I would visit the imam and ask for the statistics. In the cities, finding the people in need and intervening was more difficult.

I couldn't get access to the refugee camps in Turkey. Once I got very close and managed to talk to some people behind the wired gates in Yayladağı camp in 2012. I was around to meet the humanitarian aid convoys but the Syrian government did not let them cross the borders. We re-channeled the trucks to the checkpoint by Yayladağı in Turkey. It was when I talked to some of the camp residents through the bars but I can't consider it a real interaction. However, unlike what you read in the newspapers, I have not heard of the scandals about the exploitation of the girls and women. I should have, but I haven't.

[*The author's note: In Berkeley, I met an American woman who told me that she had access to the refugee camps in Turkey several times by bribing the guards. She brought many trays of baklawa to lift the mood and communicate with women there, which clearly made herself and the women feel better.*]

Let me tell you the story of a Syrian woman who used to live in Egypt. She met a Tunisian man with a Swiss passport through a matchmaking service which sounded similar to the annoying text message that I had received. He acted very polite at first and promised her that he'd take her and her family to Switzerland. As a first step, he rented a flat in Istanbul, performed religious marriage through an imam, but when he got satisfied with her after six months, he left for Switzerland. She got stuck in Istanbul without any Swiss visa. She contacted our initiative *Lajiaat la Sabaya* (Women Refugees not Captives) through Facebook and complained about the situation. She was unable to extend her visa for Egypt since renewing it became so difficult for Syrians that it competes with getting a U.S. visa!

The first thing I did was to cover her rent out of my own savings so that she wouldn't be on the streets. Then, I changed her phone number because I was afraid of her husband's harassment. I took care of her papers and worked really hard for her case until she made it to Sweden as a refugee. She is married to a Turkish man now. She half-jokingly encourages me to find a Turkish partner!

Redefining Home and Hope: Canada

> Among the privileges of being a refugee lawyer is helping people change their lives by obtaining protection in Canada. Yet rarely in my 27-year career have I been so moved. The 25-year-old Syrian woman recognized today by the immigration and refugee board brings honor, joy and inspiration to my heart. Is it the authenticity, the peacefulness, the passion for defending human rights? It is all of those things and more.
>
> Canada has gained a leader, who has already made a career of working for refugee protection, feminist causes and human rights. She is fluent in English and French. She exudes emotional and intellectual intelligence. She is a gem. She is on a path to being a great leader. My client is thankful to Canada but it is Canadians that should be grateful that this amazing young soul has chosen our land.
>
> —Mitchell J. Goldberg

On January 10, 2017, I found the above attachment in my email box, sent from Muzna's account. It gave me immediate goosebumps and tears. I read Muzna's lawyer's message several times and shared it with many friends and used some lines in my presentations. I wish we had more Mitchell Goldbergs on this lonely planet, who can share their feelings as open-heartedly as he did.

Regarding her asylum process and whether there were things that she wanted to criticize or improve, Muzna comments, "It is not fair to compare myself to an average refugee woman who would have language barriers to begin with. She would have no network, whereas for me, it was a different story thanks to the Nobel Women's Initiative Program in Ottawa."

In October, Muzna posted a memorable list of her impressions of Canada as a way to celebrate her first year in the country. Below is the shortened version (approved by her) of her post, which is evidence of Muzna's keen observation, hope, and a basic guideline for a better world:

> October 10th, 2017, marks my first anniversary in Canada. There is no doubt that I am a different person than the Muzna who arrived at Montréal-Trudeau Airport 365 days ago. I don't want to be the same really so the change is good. I want to share some of the highlights from my first year and also tell people that traveling is the best way to acquire new visions and ideas. It creates better and more considerate humans. I have been a blessed one considering the love and the support of my new family here, my university, my professors, my amazing friends, and my scholarship organization. I want to thank each one of them for being a part of my definition of home and hope.
>
> I may be privileged in comparison to many refugees but moving to a new country always imposes its own challenges on one's character and growth, which can result in a belonging and an identity crisis whatever that truly means.
>
> In the past 365 days, I've grown every day, become who I'm today, and I hope to

develop further. I'm still not a Canadian, but I love to think of myself as someone who reflects and contributes to the diversity of Canada.

"What Happened in the Past 365 Days?"

I've met people who willingly spent hours of their time and money by sharing them with others.

I recognized the importance of valuing a being (any species) just for its existence in the same space and time as me. And that the joy of giving is similar in all of us.

I've participated in celebrating Thanksgiving, Christmas, Passover, and I went to a Gurdwara. I can't wait to learn more about other beliefs and traditions.

I rediscovered that we humans celebrate in the same ways even when our beliefs vary, making mistreating each other meaningless.

I've met people opening doors of buildings in public and waiting for me until I reach these doors. They apologize even when they haven't done anything wrong.

I've learned how to face and discuss difficult topics, like Canada's painful colonial history of injustice and disenfranchising indigenous people, African slaves, and migrants. I wonder if other parts of the world will have a similar day (June 21st) when they celebrate diversity.

I tried Chinese, Japanese, Indian, Ethiopian, Pakistani, Greek, and Thai food. I came to believe that humans can communicate through their food and this helps breaking down barriers.

I like the taste of *poutine*, which is a Quebecois dish, but I hate its name for the obvious reason. It sounds like Putin! It is French fries with cheese and gravy sauce.

I've missed my parents, my family, and friends in Syria.

I've learned that life is about change and missing someone makes you appreciate them more.

I've met people who didn't treat me all that well and others who did so I came to the conclusion that a person's most fatal mistake is generalizing.

I've learned that nationality, gender, and religion are tiny little pieces of a person's true identity and it's up to that person to explain who they are if they want to.

For the next 365 Days, I will continue to have hopes for Canada, Syria, and the world, but only by taking the step of listening to all beings can we achieve peace. Canadians are very humble and open to other cultures. Being in Canada helped me to advance on my personal path and focus on leadership skills. It offered me a space where I live without fear.

My Approach to Religion and Feminism: Making My Way to Canada

I believe that life is change. When you have a difficult time, even if this period lasts very long, it will not last forever. I regard this challenging time as a test. After this episode is over, one begins to analyze and learn [*I tease her for sounding like a seventy-year-old than a twenty-five, she laughs*]. When the book will be out, I'll read my words and cry.

My parents are practicing Muslims. I was okay with the way Islam was practiced in my circle of friends and family. However, I no longer believe in it. It is complicated, but I will try to explain. I can no longer stand to observe the Syrian regime's using religion to exploit and control people like sheep. This whole thing affected my practice of Islam negatively and I stopped in 2014. I am aware that my idea about a gender revolution in Islam is not accepted because most people don't tolerate anyone with a different opinion. There is no liberty or democracy for us in Syria.

In fact, the role of religion in our society and politics after the Revolution affected me a lot. I cannot practice religion when I know that human morality should be demonstrated by our behavior, not by religion. We need to define ourselves as citizens first, not by a religion that we think we belong.

Many hopes and dreams that I harbor are strengthened after being in Canada. Since my arrival, I was invited to give many talks including radio programs and campus visits, and I shared my experiences across Canada as a Syrian activist and refugee. When I explain my approach to feminism, I always refer to intersectionalities and analyze the commonalities and strategies which we as Syrians share with other conflict zones such as Colombia and Iran.

I was invited to Canada because I qualified for the Nobel Women's Initiative Sister-to-Sister Mentorship Program and then applied for asylum. This program brings three young women activists to Ottawa every year for six weeks of communications and advocacy training. It was established in 2012, but the Initiative was founded earlier in 2006 by Jody Williams, Shirin Ebadi, Wangari Maathai, Rigoberta Menchú Tum, Betty Williams, and Mairead Maguire, all Nobel Peace Laureates. Their aim is to assist the women activists who work in countries around the world for peace, justice, and equality. Leymah Gbowee and Tawakkol Karman joined the Initiative in 2012. I am honored to be a part of this amazing group.

Unlike the majority of refugees, I was welcomed into a network of strong women. The idea is to share and continue with what I had started in a more stable and safe environment. Having the right kind of contacts is very important, I would claim, more important than the paper work. Starting a new life is very difficult especially with the stigma of being a refugee when it comes to finding a job or a house. I am very fortunate to be hosted by a Canadian family in Quebec. I can speak French and English, which makes life easier for me in comparison to most refugees who can't speak the language of the host country.

In Canada, I witnessed a remarkable model that I hope will be adopted by other countries, which was the private sponsorship of refugee families for one year. It is an efficient and welcoming initiative where the individuals help fulfilling the government's role or supplement it. However, we still need to remember that unless the problems on the ground are resolved, people will continue leaving Syria; and becoming a refugee is an extremely difficult situation.

We need to highlight the success stories of the newcomers to maintain hope and provide role models for Syrians as in the case of the amazing blind Syrian refugee, Hani al-Moliya. He is now a member of the National Youth Council of Canada and became a symbol for us. Hani's story reminds anyone of the refugee individuals who refuse to give up on their dreams.

When I came to Ottawa thanks to the Nobel Women's Initiative Mentorship Program, I met my new sisters from Colombia and Iran, and spent many hours speaking with them. I love the notion of sisterhood. I want feminism to be a movement where all women can take part if they choose to do so that certain women's voices are not isolated. We are privileged in one way or another and those with more privileges should work to level the playing field.

A good habit to develop is checking our privileges regularly since we are only human and nobody is perfect. We will forget our privileges sometimes because we are inherently flawed as human beings. I still have so much to learn from the global conflict prevention and peace–building work. That's why I applied to the MA programs in this field and have been accepted by Waterloo and Sherbrooke Universities. I enrolled in Conflict Resolution at Sherbrooke and began my graduate studies in fall 2017.

I continue representing Syria internationally and building peace coalitions. I flew to Korea for the Third Annual Commemoration of the September 18 World Alliance of Religions' Peace (WARP) Summit as a Syrian activist in 2017. The conference theme was "Implementation of the Declaration of Peace and Cessation of War." I visited the war memorial erected for the Canadian soldiers who served at the Korean War, connecting myself both to the history of war, the present time, and my freshly forming Syrian-Canadian identity. It was quite an experience yet you couldn't tell these complexities from my smiling face in the photographs.

Having a New Family and Sharing Visions

I got in touch with my Canadian family in Quebec thanks to a French acquaintance. His aunt's neighbors, Colleen and Marc, were hosting people through couch surfing so she thought they might also have me for a couple of days, or until I find a decent place. Well, it has been more than a year and they accepted me as part of their wonderful family of four children and a cute cat named Pistache. Colleen and Marc are a wonderful activist couple, I admire their commitment to global affairs and environmental issues.

I should have named Colleen as one of my female role models too. Every morning, I see her face and immediately feel stronger. Her energy provides my daily indoors shot of feminist empowerment. She works for an NGO named *Équiterre*, fighting for nature's rights, against pipelines and plastic consumption. In fact, she changed my life in the way that I don't use plastic anymore and I eat organic food. Marc is an amazing, hard-working man, an architect by profession, and a feminist with a big heart. We share coffee every morning. Children are either at high school or college and also working hard.

Colleen and Marc sponsored a Syrian family who arrived last year from Turkey. They reached them through UNHCR and took care of all the legal paper work to fly them over here to Canada for health treatment because the couple's both children were sick. Once the family got here, they were very supportive too and have kept in touch.

They are very humble people. I love them both so dearly that it is very hard for me to express. Colleen and Marc made my life in Canada easier and helped me to integrate smoothly, find a job, build a network, get acquainted with health system, support my physical and psychological wellbeing. I might as well have been one of their children. That's how lovingly and naturally I have been taken care of since I arrived in their home. Community is important for any displaced person no matter how privileged one may seem on the surface. I was a part of Syria, which is a site of destruction and death today. I also belong to a feminist community of women and men. My other affiliations are not as important in comparison and some of them are random or artificial such as school or extended family.

Wishing for a Normal Life? My Dreams and Interests

Among my future dreams and plans is becoming an academic, thus getting a Ph.D. after completing my MA. In ten years or so, I plan to switch to a very different occupation if life allows me, but only time will tell. I want to live in an isolated corner of the world and engage in translation and literature only. Moreover, I intend to build a voice library. I know that this may sound like an unusual dream to look forward to, but I had music training as a child and people have always told me that I have a sweet voice. I believe that hearing is more effective than seeing so this voice library will be something I will be proud to hand down such an archive.

Currently, I do my best to balance work and graduate studies. I work as an intervener at Canadian Red Cross in their refugee health program for Syrian refugees in collaboration with the Social Center for Immigrant Aid. I see this as a continuation of my work in Syria and Turkey, that is, empowering women refugees regarding their legal rights, humanitarian and logistics aid. In my limited free time, I like practicing yoga and ice-skating.

As an activist who approaches freedom and justice from a global perspective, my new area of interest in human rights is the history and the present situation of the indigenous people of Canada and their rights. After completing my own training on this burning issue, I am now helping the Syrian youth and women to understand the indigenous people's situation in Canada and how to be a part of the solutions and not of the problems in the Canadian society. As you see, I am already active in the country that welcomed me, I learn fast, and carry on activist work. I participated in Canada's National Action Plan on Women, Peace and Security 2017–2022, and gave public talks in several places including campuses and cultural centers such as the Global Studies Center of University of Victoria and *Conseil interculturel de Montréal*. I am happy to share my experiences and learn from the others, a lifelong mission.

The below passage is from a paper I wrote for one of my graduate courses, and posted on Facebook, it would be fit to include in my story:

> Refugees are always being judged by their failures. If they cannot succeed in crossing the ocean, escaping the borderline, passing an exam, finding a job, or making money, they apparently do not deserve the opportunity that has been gifted to them. They must be both heroes and victims but never normal human beings. And yet, despite this stigma, there is always a Refugees Welcome sign wherever they go and this can be very confusing.

Muzna wants a "normal" life, a word she easily used in the interview, but I have scare crows around it here. I ask for clarification, and she says, "Normal is being free from fear and guilt. I don't want to feel guilty for where I am today, but I cannot help it. Even when I drink a glass of water, I feel guilty because I know that many regions in Syria don't have drinking water or electricity."

As for her commitment to a relationship with a man, I had the fortune of witnessing what Muzna meant by a joint 24/7 participation to a mission. Else, she feels, the relation will crumble in one way or another. If she had a partner who wanted to spend his Sunday afternoon away from everything but Muzna, he would have to deal with certain challenges. Intervening a domestic violence case and reaching people in charge demanded urgency which I humbly contributed on a Sunday afternoon in fall 2016. In fact, I remember vividly the colorful nursery in Berkeley where I received her text, in the middle of many flowers and citrus scions.

The below dialogues are presented as examples to a transformational bond, which was feminist in nature, between the researcher-writer and the co-participant.

Muzna: Hi Ozlem! I need to get in touch with one of your colleagues or friends who works at a shelter in Istanbul.

OE: Hey, how are you? What's the story? I'll do my best. The oldest one is called Mor Çatı, which was in Beyoğlu, Taksim. They are very experienced.

M: Can you give me their number? It is an urgent case.

OE: I'll try to reach someone, but let me give you their hotline number. Remember that it is 10 p.m. in Turkey now. Let's hope my friend can respond.

M: This is a case with a Syrian woman with three daughters. Her husband kicked them out after beating her up violently so we need protection for her and for children in a shelter.

OE: I'll see what I can do. When are you returning to Istanbul?

M: I will finish the program here and look for scholarship in Canada to continue my studies. I am not returning.

OE: I understand. I am just surprised. Did you know that I lived and studied in Toronto?

M: Really?

OE: Yes, I got my Ph.D. from York University, Gender and Women's Studies.

M: Wow! No, I didn't. I'm looking for opportunities here too since my passport will expire this year. I don't have many options but to stay :(

OE: Keep in touch, I can introduce you to some women at York. Good luck.

After this online conversation, I found the address and phone number of Mor Çatı Women's Shelter but could not reach the friend I had in mind. Muzna thanked me, passed the information forward and sent me the following link about the program where she was interviewed by an Oxfam staff: http://www.huffingtonpost.ca/Oxfam-Canada/women-girls-refugee-crisis_ b_12142712.html.

I congratulated Muzna and told that in case she decided to apply to York, I would definitely mention this life interview project in my reference letter. She checked with me to see how far I was able to proceed with the women refugee interviews for the book. She had a genuine interest from the beginning since she provided me several names and emails so that I could reach more activist women of Syria.

Muzna sent me another link and informed me about her talk at the Center for Global Studies in University of Victoria, entitled "Responses to the Refugee Crisis" on October 17, 2016. Her picture and first name were printed on the event poster as "the special guest." I asked her if I could include the poster in my slides for my talk at the Institute of European Studies at UC Berkeley. "Sure, you can use whatever you want" was the immediate response with a smiley. We also exchanged information about our upcoming trips and my interviews in Germany and Sweden. In less than a few days, she shared the contact information of five more Syrian women in case I wanted to meet them.

In mid–December 2016, Muzna sent her condolences to me after the bombings and the civilian losses in Beşiktaş and Maçka, Istanbul. She was working as an interpreter at a church for Syrian refugees and accepted a new position in an NGO called Bassamat. It was an empowerment project for Syrian women in Canada and she sounded excited about it. But she also said she missed Istanbul. I mentioned my long-term dream of interviewing her, maybe ten years from today after she becomes an established academic and activist with dual citizenship. Maybe we will choose Istanbul for realizing this project.

In mid–January 2017, we exchanged messages about her MA applications. She was full of new plans and busy as ever. However, after January, Muzna stopped our communication. She did not give me any excuses and it took me a while to hear back even after sending her a series of emails and WhatsApp texts, almost begging for an update. I felt like a parent, irrationally worrying about her daughter. Because of her straightforward and bold tone in her anti-government postings and her immediate family being all over the world now, I got worried about her safety. My concerns were part of the life inquiry process and I like to make my personal feelings as a writer traceable into this narrative. Each co-participant has her own immediate family and circle of close friends, who were obviously their priority. Still, I expected them to respond in a week or so, and when they didn't, I became worried about their wellbeing.

In mid–February, after a month of silence, Muzna sent me a reference letter request, which I immediately submitted to University of Waterloo. She applied to the MA in Peace and Conflict Studies there. Then the silence resumed and lasted much longer than the first one until I finally got some news from her in July 2017. Her e-mail was different, and she said that something had happened to her old Gmail account. I was glad to be in touch again since her story needed fact checks before going to the publishing house. This time, she was prompt and clarified several issues in her interviews. We are planning to meet in Canada in 2019 and attend a panel together where we share our experiences of life recording and feminist activism across cultures and continents. In October 2017, Muzna flew to Paris to launch the Syrian Women's Political Movement, which was one of her dreams regarding the politics in Syria. She carries Syria in her mind and heart all the time regardless of the thousands of miles of distance where she currently lives. She repeated several times that her personal success story does not palliate the pain caused by the horrible things in Syria which she has been very closely following every day.

4

Sama's Story
What I Survived
Were My Eye-Openers

I was born in Damascus on January 9, 1989. The earliest memory I have is playing with colorful pieces of Legos. The same bricks sometimes became a boat and then transformed into a tree or a house. I have four siblings, two sisters and two brothers. My cousins are also like brothers and sisters to me.

I remember a pleasant daily ritual from my childhood. My uncle took us every morning to the small local patisserie for some cookies before heading to his office. My grandfather visited us every Friday, his pockets were full of candies. We lined up from the youngest to the eldest, knowing that he would only give them away in this particular order, always beginning with the youngest.

We lived on a big family farm until it was time for us to go to school. My siblings and my cousins must have looked like a gang of dwarves. Each family had its own unit on the farm but we grew up together. My grandmother used to tell us stories and fairytales while we were in bed. We always asked for more before giving into sleep. We watched TV too. My favorite animations were Heidi, Vikings, and Lady Oscar. The last one has a very interesting main character. Lady Oscar acts like a man, she wants to be a warrior for the Queen of France. I also remember watching Sesame Street. I still recall the songs in it, and sometimes we sing them with my cousins just to laugh or feel nostalgic.

We used to go to picnics in my father's car, which almost always proved to be too small for the family trips. We were all on top of each other, singing songs along the way, we had so much fun. It is hard to conceive that the farm house is no longer there. Everything was damaged, even the trees died because of the war.

We lived in the countryside for more than ten years until my maternal grandfather told my mother one day that he wanted to share his house in Damascus, which would offer better opportunities to his grandchildren. After giving it some thought, my parents agreed and we moved to the city but kept the house and the farm in the country to spend the summers. We lived in Damascus until my grandfather died when I was in tenth grade.

My parents enrolled me in a private Islamic school so that I could get a good education and learn the Quran. I have very unpleasant memories of that school due to their harsh discipline except for the first day. I remember holding my father's hands and taking my seat in the classroom. He reassured me that he would come back to pick me up afterward. The first day was lovely. However, several children were crying and it didn't make sense to me.

Our female-only educator team had mean ways of dealing with students. They didn't spare insulting words to humiliate us, and they used sticks to punish us physically at times. Our uniforms had to be in perfect condition just like our fingernails. It was like military and prison at the same time. That's also where I began learning English but never had a chance to practice it until our forced displacement in 2014.

Then, we moved back to the countryside in 2003 and lived there until 2012. I don't recall having problems during my childhood except that I had gluten allergy. I couldn't eat any bread, for example. I became the favorite child because of this problem. Our relatives used to tell my mother not to restrict my diet, but she replied, "I love her more than anything and I want her to be healthy; it is for her own good."

Thanks to my mother and our family doctor who prepared a gluten-free diet for me, I remained healthy. When I turned twelve, Mom organized a nice birthday party, which took place at my grandparents' house. I invited all my classmates and had a great time. My allergy disappeared when I turned eighteen and my mother was very happy.

I feel very fortunate to have grown up in a happy, supportive, extended family on the countryside. My parents never inflicted any physical punishment on me or any of my four siblings. Not even once! I can't believe some adults can beat their children, it is unacceptable.

The happiest time of my life was when my sister had her first daughter, it was amazing! I can't express the love I hold for my niece. I saw the baby minutes after she was born when the nurse washed her for the first time. My brother-in-law was in tears.

My sister had another daughter recently. Each time I see my nieces, I think of doing something good for society. I want to adopt an orphan, for example. I discussed it with my parents. I was in Syria then but we needed to move to Lebanon. My family differs from other Syrian families because I can have discussions with my parents and siblings about things that most families can't discuss. Especially my mom can listen to me for hours and shares her opinions. My dad looks tough from outside, but he cries at almost all the sad movies we see.

2011 and After: The March Demonstrations and Redefining "Hero"

I remember vividly the time when the Tunisian dictator Ben Ali resigned and fled the country in mid–January 2011 after twenty-three years in power! I was very happy and surprised, but what followed in Egypt was even more incredible when Mubarak resigned and fled Cairo on February 11, 2011. It was one of the biggest historical events of my life. We lost my paternal grandfather only three days before Mubarak's resignation. I felt awful because he was waiting for Mubarak to fall. He was very vocal in his criticism and grief about all the innocent people who were killed by the regime.

On the day of the demonstrations in March 2011, I was at work, but after the news, I could no longer focus on anything like everyone else. I left the office early and came home. We watched the news on TV together as a family. I was surprised, horrified, and happy, all at the same time. It was the most complicated feeling. My whole family had similar feelings. It was just an unbelievable and magnificent event.

My parents did not let us participate in the demonstrations. They were very strict about it and even today, I feel like a coward for not attending. In fact, the only thing that I don't feel good about the demonstrations is my failure to join them. I believe my siblings will also continue having the same sentiment. We all knew that it was very dangerous. People got killed or detained, sometimes only because their names were confused with others on the Syrian government's list.

All communications were monitored by the officers regardless of one's location. Even in Lebanon or Turkey, many Syrians were afraid to post remarks online because they had family left in Syria who could suffer from these anti-government statements. In short, I have not witnessed the horrible events that most Syrians had to go through, so I can be considered fortunate in that way. You asked me whether I had any heroes, well, I didn't understand the real meaning of hero until 2011. Then I saw a lot of young people who stood unarmed on the streets so courageously and chanted "freedom, freedom!" They are the anonymous heroes of my life.

Our Flight from Violence and Injustice

It is hard to talk about certain experiences and feelings in detail but suffice to say that leaving Syria was a difficult decision. Our first stop in 2014 was Lebanon where we lived at a large house with my sister and her husband. They were living there already for some time. Our family unification felt nice, but finding a job and getting residency proved to be more difficult than we had imagined. When the authorities didn't renew our visas, we decided to move to Turkey in November 2015. My brothers already left for Germany in August 2015, which was one of the hardest memories that I have. We didn't know if we would see them again. My mother cried a lot and my father hid behind his sunglasses when he hugged both my brothers.

We had no house to live in Turkey but our relatives hosted us very kindly. Our efforts to find jobs and a proper place to live failed after a month-long search. I wouldn't mind staying in Turkey, I really liked it there. It was mainly my mother who insisted that we go to Germany. She couldn't bear the idea of being separated from her sons for long. She also argued that Germany would offer us better education opportunities and a brighter future in the long term.

The Turkish government is the first and the only country which began granting nationality to Syrians so far. We have some friends in Turkey, who already got residency and became citizens. The Lebanese government caused more difficulties for us in comparison. My younger sister wanted to go to high school in Lebanon, but she was told that she lacked the proper papers. When she saw her friends' high school graduation pictures posted online in Syria, she became very upset. She was the only one in her class who couldn't graduate. She is twenty years old and still trying to finish her high school in Germany.

Speaking of which, if the conflict continues, many Syrian children will have no nationality and no education. This is a growing problem about which I am very concerned. I wish I could do something about it. As far as the statistics go, the average time out of a country for a refugee is over a decade, which means, thousands of refugee children may reach adulthood without enjoying any schooling. Then, I read other disturbing, more recent statistics on Syrian refugees specifically which show high rates of child marriage among girls and child labor among boys and girls. No wonder most parents decide to risk a deadly voyage to Europe. I believe it's for their children's education more than anything. Anyway, I was talking about our time when we decided to head to Germany to live with my brothers. The first step was to find a smuggler to take us to Greece across the Aegean.

The boldest thing I have ever done is to take the ferry from Turkey to Greece not only because it was illegal but also because I don't know how to swim. If something happened to the ferry, that was it. I'd be long gone. It was me, my younger sister, and my parents. My mother was overwhelmed by the fear of drowning and kept crying for hours. The smugglers lied to us, like they did to hundreds of refugees, and told us that the journey would be safe and comfortable. They showed us the picture of a yacht instead of the small boat that we found ourselves in with more than forty people. The scene was unimaginable.

This chapter of our lives showed us the dark side of Turkey. We couldn't believe the type of people we ended up dealing with. We were so naïve and afraid of what we were about to do at the time so when the smugglers forced us into the boat, we reluctantly agreed. They threatened us that they'd call the Turkish police if we failed to step in. It didn't occur to us at that shocking moment that if *they* called the police, they'd be in jail for life. *We* should have called the police, not them! The decision to step into that boat after wasting a lot of money was a "now or never" moment. My mother was convinced that the boat would sink and we would all die, no words of consolation helped her.

We got on the boat and started the cell phone's GPS to follow what was going on. The crossing felt like the longest journey of my life. However, we finally arrived on the Greek island of Samos and felt so grateful to Allah that we survived this very dangerous undertaking. There was not a single living soul around. We tried to start a fire, hoping that someone would see and rescue us. Once we accepted that the fire plan was not working, we decided to walk as a group until we ran into someone. After one hour or so, not having seen anyone, I came up with an idea and asked around if anyone's phone had Internet. Only one young man answered positively and let me use his phone. I called 112 [*equivalent to 911*] and explained to the person on the other end of the connection that we, a group of forty or so Syrians, are somewhere on an island, which seemed completely deserted and we needed immediate help. I was told that the rescue team was on their way soon.

After fifteen minutes, two buses arrived to pick us up. In addition to the officers, there were several doctors from the organization "Doctors Without Borders." Everyone was very kind and they eventually took us to a refugee camp. From where we were to the camp lasted only about fifteen minutes by bus. Once at the camp, we were registered as refugees and we received a picture ID within two days, which allowed us to move on to the next country. First, we took a ferry to Athens, then a bus to the Greek border, and proceeded to Macedonia. From there, we took a taxi to Serbia where we got on a train to Croatia. We had to transfer trains before arriving in Germany, but at least we didn't cross any new borders.

We had to protect our new picture IDs at all costs because it was the only official document which proved our status and prior stops. If you lose it, you'd be detained in the next border control. In total, we were on the road for ten days of December 2015. I would say it was uneventful and I can't think of anything that stands out in my memory for the moment.[1] Except that…. The heating system of the bus from Athens to the Greek border was broken. We were freezing for hours even though the bus was completely full.

When we finally stepped on the German soil, we were welcomed in English by two German officers, who acted like the kindest souls on the planet. I can never forget their polite treatment, I just can't. I wish I see them again one day and express my gratitude in proper words.

Sometimes here in Germany, when we chat with other Syrians, they warn us that the civilized behavior of the Germans is only on the surface and temporary, but I don't believe them. I take my own experience with Germans as a criterion beginning with the initial border crossing, dealing with the paper work, all of which were handled with kindness, and nothing else.

Let me show you some pictures [*she takes out her phone*]. These are the pictures of some German friends whom I met in Darmstadt. There are always volunteers around, who want to meet and assist us, the new comers, in order to ease our tension and transition challenges.

The most important lesson I have learned after what I had been through can be summarized in two sentences: Nothing is completely good or completely bad. Similarly, nobody is completely right or completely wrong in this life. When I go to sleep, I still have many dreams and some nightmares which take place in Syria. Sometimes, I am concerned that I may never be able to go back.

Graduation Under the Bombs

I had to quit university just before my very last semester when the family decided to leave Syria for Lebanon. It simply became too dangerous to attend the classes although we were supposed to be there only on Fridays and Saturdays. It is called "Open University" so its schedule was different than regular ones. However, Fridays were the days of the large demonstrations, which also meant violent police response. My mother forbid me to attend classes and said I could only go out during the exam days to finish the university.

One day, a heavy bombardment began near our neighborhood in Damascus and we barely escaped it. After surviving that horrible attack, we moved to my grandparents' house in the country and stayed there for a while. I no longer attended the university then. From their house, we left for Lebanon, but I was very determined to get my degree no matter what. My father agreed to drive me back to Damascus for the next semester and picked me up in April. During these two months, I stayed at my uncle's house whose family were very kind to me. They are like my parents. I got my diploma from the Translation Department in April 2014.

My uncle is one of few people who stayed in Damascus. He is a lawyer and a big lover of the ancient city. He told us that he is like a fish, and Damascus is his sea. He cannot breathe if he leaves. I personally feel guilty that I left Syria without doing anything for my country. I hope to go back one day as a successful citizen and serve there. For example, I can adopt children, and if I have enough money, I can build hospitals, schools, etcetera.

My best friend Zein is also my youngest aunt, and was my classmate in the Translation Department. She stayed in Syria, finished her degree, and is now working as an English teacher. It was very hard to say goodbye, but we communicate everyday by phone. She is only one year younger than I am. Sometimes I feel that she is the reason for my becoming a translator. After high school, I wanted to study English Literature, but I couldn't perform well enough in the baccalaureate exam. Then, we both enrolled in the open university. Zein's brother, fifteen years her senior, told her in 2009, "You have five years maximum to complete your degree, so you better study hard." She did! She has a stronger personality than I do, and I admire her straightforwardness. Maybe it is related to the fact that she lost her father when she was thirteen, a time when everybody began intervening in her behavior. She stood against it, which made her stronger.

On Practices of Islam and Sama's Suitors' First Quiz

I believe we used to be more religious in Syria. I began wearing the hijab at eighth grade [*Sama shows me a picture of herself without the headscarf, taken in Damascus a few years ago right after a haircut*]. I wish I could invest more time in Islam. However, we need to acquire different skills and learn many things in our new lives here. Learning German is my top priority. All these adaptation and survival efforts are also distractions from my religion. I also know that Islam demands its followers to work hard. It is not enough to post "pray for Syria" notes online, we should do something.

The Prophet Mohammed once said, "A strong believer is better and dearer to Allah than a weak one, and both are good." In this hadith, goodness as a virtue is acknowledged in weak and in strong people because the true faith is a common feature of both followers. However, the strong ones are better because they are more active and energetic in performing ritual prayers and noble deeds in life, whether obligatory or not.

My younger sister and I have many conversations about religion. She keeps asking me countless questions and I do my best to come up with reasonable answers. I shared with her that the acts of worship is not the whole matter in religion and we should use our minds to find God by our own unique way.

Every evening, when we sit down to have dinner as a family, the interpretations of Islam dominate our conversations. Thanks to the open-minded parents who raised me, I can stand up for my own interpretations and have objections sometimes. To support my points, I show them references from the Quran in my phone. My father also follows different interpretations of the passages from our holy book and uses the laptop at home. I enjoy these conversations, and I want to become more religious in time. I never miss my daily prayers and prefer to practice them in solitude if I can. Sometimes I am afraid to lose my faith all of a sudden. I seek refuge in God and say, "God, please make my faith stronger."

I don't claim that questioning our religion is bad but where do we find the answers? Everyone has a different opinion and come up with another interpretation. When I decide to pose a question, and receive a reply back, I don't know if this person is right or wrong. Indeed, we have many *murshids* and sheikhs in Syria, some really gave good advice and taught us virtuous things. However, when the revolution started, most of them sided with the dictator so the youth lost faith in them, which is a problem. Sheikh Mohammad Said Ramadan al-Buti whose books we used to read and discuss was one of them. My aunt and I used to attend his lectures at the mosque in Damascus. One night in 2013, he was killed along with twenty people in the mosque after a suicide attack. It was reported later that the regime killed him, and even accused him of being on the oppositional side, I don't know.

We always celebrate the end of Ramadan, Eid al Adha, and the birth of Muhammad, *mawlid*. Sometimes we prepare a milk pudding and serve it to our guests. We don't celebrate birthdays regularly but turning to twenty-five felt special for me, more like an adult. We baked a cake and had a mini celebration among the family. Our most important family tradition is having dinner every evening where we all get together and share a meal. It provides me a strong sense of comfort and belonging. I also feel that I am part of a larger Syrian community because I have very strong feelings about the situation in the country. True that I care about humanity in general, but my priority would be to serve to my country whenever I have the chance.

When someone phones my parents with the intention of marrying me or my younger sister, one of the first questions that my father asks him is, "Do you practice religion?" It is the initial test that the suitor needs to pass before coming to our house with his parents [*Sama is laughing*]. Just for the record, I don't know why but we received so many marriage proposals since we got here. My guess is that there are hardly any young men left in Syria today.

[*I ask Sama if she feels comfortable sharing more about these suitors. She nods but asks me to turn off the recorder. Thus, she tells me some stories from the past and the present. Her ideas about the men-women relations can be best traced by the novels she reads and recommends, which I am allowed to write here.*]

On Literature and Marriage

I enjoy reading love stories, especially the ones with challenges, which make the bond between the two lovers even stronger and more passionate. There is one novel that I really loved, called *Birds of the South* by Amani Abul Fadl. An Egyptian man goes to the U.S. to study and falls in love with his new friend's sister, who is from Iraq. However, he is Sunni and she is Shia. Something really shocking happens on the night of their wedding. I read the novel many times. I believe the author is very sensitive about human rights, the sectarian violence, and discrimination.

I also truly enjoyed reading *Forty Rules of Love* by Elif Shafak. The main character is an unhappily married Jewish housewife named Ella who lives in the U.S. Through a book named *Sweet Blasphemy* by Aziz Zahara, she learns about Shams of Tabriz, who was the mentor and close friend of Rumi in the thirteenth century. Over the course of their email exchanges, Ella is transformed, and realizes in time that she is ready to give up her life for him. Shams' lessons or rules of love affect her deeply and I was very impressed by Ella's courage.

Nizar Kabbani is my favorite poet. Based on his poems, I imagine him to be the perfect lover to whoever he gives his heart away. Some Lebanese and Syrian vocalists used his poems as lyrics to their songs. There are two reasons for my admiration for him. Although he lived in London for decades, our capital city remained in his poems, such as "The Jasmine Scent of Damascus." Secondly, his anti-authoritarianism, which reflects a different face of this romantic and sensual poet. "O Sultan, my master, if my clothes are ripped and torn, it is because your dogs with claws are allowed to tear me" is often quoted because of Syrians' frustration with the life under the dictatorship. Kabbani met his second wife at a poetry recital in Baghdad. She was killed in a bomb attack by pro–Iranian terrorists in Beirut. She was a teacher but worked in Beirut at the time for the cultural affairs of Iraq. I can't imagine the pain of losing your lover in such a horrible way. He wrote a very long poem after her death called "Balqis," which you can find online.

I believe marriage to be an important and exciting experience. Respect and sharing common interests are the two main elements that exist in every long-lasting marriage as far as I can observe and hear from other people. Like any human experience, it can't be measured and each person will have her or his own experience. The ideal married couple I have in mind is my friend Fairuz and her husband Sami because they are open about everything. They even designated one hour per week to comment on each other's behavior without bad feelings. I like observing their relationship, and I wish they continue this way.

In April 2017, I got engaged to Jad, who is also from Damascus. He came to Germany by himself from Syria in September 2015 and has been living in Bingen am Rhein since then, not far from Frankfurt. He asked his family in Damascus to connect him to the Syrian families in Germany in order to meet a potential wife. His mother reached out to my mother and they talked on the phone about introducing us. That's how we met. He came over to our house, met my parents, and we went out for 4–5 times. We spent hours talking so that we could get to know each other. We felt that the marriage would work.

Jad went to Paris to buy our rings, which was a kind gesture. We had a modest engagement ceremony. He is a calm person and his rational side is stronger than his emotions. I think most men are like that. He studied electrical engineering and worked in a company in Damascus for ten years. He has four sisters, one is older, the other three are younger than him. My ideal life picture, which is unlikely to appear in near future, includes opening my translation office in Damascus and a cute healthy baby. Currently [*October 2017*], we are still looking for a house to rent, but it is very difficult to find one in Germany.

About My Personality and My Hero in the Family

I have always had a lot of questions regarding History, I don't even know where to begin. Who was the first person on the planet? How were the empires formed? Now I want to know more about the Middle East and the history of Islam. When I lived in Damascus, I thought the whole world was Damascus. Then, I saw many other women from different cities and countries. In Syria, I thought we were all Arabs. Now I know that there have been Kurds, Assyrians, Yazidis, and Christians too. I am finally aware of the diversity within my country. I think if each woman receives a good education we will be stronger and more open-minded. Anyone who is educated has better control of her life.

I am not the type of person who holds on to regrets. I prefer to look ahead and make plans. I want to study journalism as a second degree because I met journalists in Syria who came from different Western countries to report the war news. I was fascinated by their bold pursuit of truth and their desire to report it under the most challenging circumstances. I can't fully grasp the urge, especially when the events are taking place in another country, but I want to experience it myself. I am shy but I would like to gain more self-confidence in time.

After I got engaged in April 2017 and began making marriage plans, I am longer so sure about studying journalism. I also have doubts about adopting children since it might be challenging to convince Jad about it. Only time will tell.

My older brother Amir, with whom I share almost the identical birthdays (he was born on January 8) tells me that women like to receive sympathy and that's why I like Germans. He is an educated, diligent man, and definitely my hero. He has a degree in Economics and worked very hard for two years to build his business in Lebanon. However, the authorities did not provide him the residency papers so he considers his time and intense labor in Lebanon a total waste.

I value Amir's opinions a lot. After three years in Germany, he was the last person in our family to receive his papers. This delay kept his young wife apart from him for all this time. The rest of us were done with our paper work which allow us to work although we arrived in Germany later than he had. In fact, it was due to the family reunification policy that we were granted the right to be here. I remember my mother's begging the German officer on the border to be united with her sons whom she hasn't seen for years.

Finally, on December 27, 2016, Amir also became official and our family was very relieved. His wife had been waiting in Lebanon to join him for almost three years but the paper work takes forever sometimes. They decided to get a divorce in early 2018. She must have been very frustrated by the separation, not knowing when to receive the news on her visa, and also told him that she didn't want to live in Germany. With God's willing, starting new families in near future won't be too complicated since they don't have any children. There is a reason behind everything so I believe whatever happened was for their own good in the long run.

5

Emilia's Story
I Change Every Moment and Am Fine with It

Emilia and I settled comfortably in a cozy café in Toronto. Warmth of fresh coffee and pastries posed a nice contrast to the cold November weather outside. We chose a small table and I felt relieved to realize that she was talkative and friendly. Her life story began to unfold smoothly:

I was born on June 20, 1988, raised in a Sunni-Muslim family in Homs. I was the last child and the only girl of five siblings. I wasn't told anything unusual about my birth except that my mother didn't want me because I was a girl. I still tease her about it, and she always clarifies that it was only because she knew how difficult girls' lives in Syria were. Fortunately, I turned out to be a good baby. She also told me that I always had this very confident personality and that I treated people as if they all worked for me. However, all I can remember was feeling desperate to have friends other than my Barbie. I used to make clothes for her.

My mom must have been overwhelmed with raising five children. When I was seven, my father left us. Before this happened, my father and I were very close as I was his little favorite girl. But he was traveling all the time because he was a long-distance truck driver. In the rare times that he was at home, he fought with Mom due to financial problems.

My mother was vocal about his irresponsible behavior toward us, and he reacted back. My father used to take me to men-only gatherings which made my mom very upset. She felt that he was exposing me to adult men. She turned out to be right since the first sexual harassment that I can recall was inflicted by one of my father's friends when I was six.

We were kicked out of our house when I was eight. After that, my mother struggled to find a place to rent. We changed many houses. Our extended family members never helped us except my mother's brother, but that wasn't much. She worked hard until we were teenagers. We dropped out of school to help her with the rent and food. I recall my mom always being tired and complaining about aches. I believe her sadness turned into physical pain. She loved us, but she was unable to express her emotions in an embodied way, so I am not used to getting hugs or things like that. She was strong but with a broken soul. Heavy smoking deteriorated her heart and lungs. We used to take her to the hospital occasionally. I often slept on the sound of her crying at night.

I was twelve when my dad returned in search of some money from his family. But he left after a few months, and never came back. It didn't hurt me much because he wasn't really there in the first place. As early as I can remember, my mom was the one managing the household and my father was away traveling. Between the ages of thirteen and eighteen, it became obvious that I didn't agree with how my mom handled things. She wanted my father back, and so did my oldest brother. I saw their attitude as naive since my father had never cared about us. I knew that he wasn't coming back, so why bother about him and create expectations? My stance distanced me from my mother and brothers as they saw my response as a cold-hearted one. My oldest brother was always abusive to all of us at home, so I stood against him. Each time I did that, the rest of them eventually made up, and I ended up as the outsider.

My mother never used physical punishment. She was very powerful and all of us feared her. Maybe we were afraid to make her sad, but she didn't realize it. She thought we never appreciated her, but at least for me, it was the opposite. I was worshipping my mom! However, I was also quite a rebel, so much so that the school quickly lost its appeal and at the age of fourteen, I decided that it was not my place to hang out.

I learned English from the movies. In fact, I recall discovering that I understood everything in a movie without subtitles when I was sixteen or seventeen. I found a job as an administrative assistant at Petro-Canada Company in Syria. My English got better as I worked there, since I could practice what I had heard at the movies. As I made my way to Canada after some episodes in Yemen where I worked less than a month, Dubai (late November 2011, stayed for six months), Jordan (May 2012), Lebanon (late December 2012) my English improved.

Inheritance and Education Come in Different Guises

My mom's father was originally from Aleppo, and my father's wealthy grandfather was among the first families in Homs records. I have heard people's saying that my paternal grandfather was a Jew from Lebanon and that when he came to Syria, he converted to Islam. But I am not sure if this is true or just gossip.

I inherited my mother's generosity, smartness, loyalty, charm, compassion, even her body smell, and many body features. She is strong but won't use it in any unjust manner. For example, she resigned from the Baath Party on the basis of her moral values. She never attended their meetings during her years in college. The imposition of the government's politics was something she resisted at a young age.

Our family was different from others because we were the only family headed by a single mother who was not a widow or divorced. My mom was not a gossip. She rarely had contacts with the neighbors; we were mostly on our own. I have never met someone whose family kept it so much to itself. First of all, the husband's abandonment is rare. If it ever occurred, then the extended family would help. In our case, we rarely received any support.

My mom taught me generosity and independence. She often trusted me to do things on my own. She told me not to consider a relationship unless I truly love someone. When Syria descended into a civil war, she told me that people who love us can do terrible things, thinking they are doing the right things. I also learned from her that I can never change anyone without their commitment to change. I have always been a straightforward person, so I value honesty, directness, sharing, and caring for those in my life. I try to stay true to myself.

I acquired my father's love of travel, argumentative skills, and fear of commitment. I used to feel a bit jealous of people with good grandparents. Now, I also have elder friends who are like family to me so I no longer feel that way.

I don't ask for help, so people rarely offer it, including my own family. I didn't feel nurtured as a child, because I was always viewed as a strong girl. As the only girl among the siblings, I was not necessarily close to my brothers. I often had to like the sports that they enjoyed to get a chance of having fun with them. One of my brothers was quite obsessed with video games, so I played those games (Atari!) as a pastime. In time, we grew apart. If my family had had the money, I would have liked attending a dance school as a child. I love dancing.

My maternal grandparents often made us feel like outsiders. They always helped my uncle's children with schoolwork and other things, but not us. I frequently questioned my mom's motive to keep any relation with them, so I grew distant as I got older. I had contact with my relatives only for my mother's sake. After I rebelled against my mother and brothers, I cut off my ties completely.

My major struggles as a child were helping my mom to feel herself better, making friends, and getting along with my brothers and school. The most significant event in my life before puberty was my father's abandonment because it was considered a dreadful shame for women in the society. In our case, it also meant being on the streets. Seeing my mom's suffering was bad enough. I never felt like a teenager because of assuming all these responsibilities since I was eight.

After my father left us, I was mostly concerned with helping my mother. The only pastime activities that I can recount were watching films at home and going to the supermarket to get stuff for the house. I used to love playing on the streets, but it wasn't appropriate for girls to be out playing with boys around after we turned eleven or twelve. As a teenager, I had not even once been to a café; we had no money to waste.

However, I had daydreams. Dreaming didn't cost anything, and I wasn't punished for them. I always thought that I was going to have a very adventurous life. Someone powerful and handsome would fall in love with me. I remember dreaming that people would admire me because I'd be very clever, speak many languages, look very glamorous in smart clothes. I'd support my family financially. Furthermore, I'd be involved in a secret mission! These dreams slowly began wearing out in time because I was barely surviving and I had to deal with painful realities of life.

My first memory of attending school was feeling alone and isolated since I was hardly able to make friends. My early school years were okay; I didn't fail any classes. My classmates often didn't like me because I was pretty, something which girls hated and boys didn't feel comfortable with. I didn't have a favorite teacher or class, and I don't have fond memories of school in general. The worst one was when a teacher in my secondary school called me poor, as if it was a sin because I didn't have the appropriate school shoes. After this incident, I dropped out of school. I also wanted to work and help my mother with the money situation. I didn't believe that school was useful anyway. However, today, I am proud to be detoured into the education at a Canadian university as a young adult with little help from anyone.

On Women's Reputation

In theory, opposite sex interactions are accepted in Syria, but only if they are to become official in the future. In practice, people have never approved of relations between boys and girls. My male friends always told me that I was stupid to risk my reputation as a girl for talking to the boys. The same friends also knew that I didn't care. My mother and brothers did! I remember sometimes my male friends didn't walk with me in public for my own sake. I chose them carefully, so whenever I needed help, it was my friends who helped me, not my family. My mother never approved of my hanging out with the opposite sex.

When I left Syria and came to Dubai in late 2011, I realized that my definition of a liberated woman did not match with the people I met in Dubai. Being a free woman for them was superficially perceived and badly misunderstood. This was the main reason why I wanted to leave Dubai as soon as possible. If one hangs out with men at the bars, she is a liberated woman. Nothing could be further from the truth than that. I don't even smoke, let alone other things.

A woman, who is free from religion or other doctrines, needs to establish her own set of ethical values and hold on to them. She has to take full responsibility for her actions and use her reason well. This may cause her to be stricter and more disciplined than most other women who may not seem half as liberal. I look independent and free-spirited, but it doesn't mean that I am "available."

I value sexual freedom, by which I simply mean having the liberty of wearing what I want to wear, and most importantly, not putting any intrinsic value on virginity. My ideas are considered inappropriate in the Syrian culture. Whoever I sleep with should be my personal choice, not a matter of honor among family, religion or society.

I hate alcohol or other stuff which clouds human reasoning and authentic individuality. I don't want to be dependent on something to enjoy or tolerate my life. I think the first time I ever drank was in my early twenties. Before that, I simply didn't have any interest. I am not uptight about it either; it depends on the company. As for smoking, I find it disgusting.

My father's abandonment was the most significant event in my life. Well, the second most weighty incident is the sexual assault that happened in Yemen in April 2010. Let me try to summarize my conclusions from this unfortunate occurrence. First, choosing the people you hang out with can be fatal; I can't even bring myself to call them "friends" in this case. Second, I lost trust in the Syrian officials including the embassy, and I distrust Arabs in general as colleagues after what happened. Finally, there is the double standard of morality when it comes to women's sexuality.

Let me rewind a bit. After having a serious argument with my mom due to my sister-in-law's finding a pregnancy test in my room, I ended up at the hospital to prove that I was still a virgin. My mother told me to leave because she didn't want a whore in her house. I told her that I would prove her wrong and then leave the house. The hospital thing was awful, but what I had told my family was verified, and I kept my word about leaving home.

Since Yemen didn't require a visa from Syrians, I left immediately for work. The only way for me to survive was to take the receptionist position at the hotel in Yemen where I was raped. You can imagine how guilty my mother must have felt after I gave her the news.

My best friend in Homs had introduced me to a girl who joined me to work at the same hotel with her boyfriend. I witnessed her lying to other people about her job, family, religious practices so I never liked her. But there we were, suddenly in Yemen as colleagues.

I minded my own business there. The girl was acting weird. One day, she knocked on my door and wanted to sleep in the bed next to me because she was afraid. The next day she was not even talking to me! The hotel owner told me that I was different from this girl and her boyfriend because they were slackers. He invited me to hang out with him and chew *qat* with his friends, which I turned down. This chewing *qat* was a very common addiction for men in Yemen, which I didn't know.

Surviving Sexual Assault

Now that I think about it, I was so ignorant. I was only twenty-one, so upset and so angry with my mother. I arrived in Yemen without even making a proper Internet search. I would have noticed many warning signs if I had. The hotel owner fired both the girl and her boyfriend after only twenty days of our arrival. He raped me on the twenty first day. Having the master keys to all the rooms, he simply unlocked my door and did his thing, only to realize that I was a virgin. This girl and her boyfriend told him that I exchanged sex for money so he was shocked when he saw the blood. When he was doing it, I was thinking how to run away. He had a plan. He would give me some money to undergo the reconstructive virginity surgery and I would continue working at his hotel. I knew only one other person in Yemen, a taxi driver named Hasan, who picked me from the airport. I called him and told him that I needed his help immediately.

The hotel owner was right outside the hotel when Hasan arrived. Because I had nothing with me except my phone, he assumed that I'd come back. Hasan took me to the hospital, and the moment I entered, I fainted. I don't remember well but I think I was crying too. The feeling I had after the rape was as if someone had pulled out all my organs. Fortunately, Hasan stayed with me. He proved to be such a nice and trustworthy guy. He was only nineteen at the time, living with his mother in a small house.

When I finally gained consciousness at the hospital, I couldn't believe my eyes. The hotel owner was standing next to me. The staff had called him because his number happened to be the first on the call-list. I screamed at him and told the staff what had happened while he ran away. They then asked about Hasan, and I told them he was my friend and I wanted him to stay. Both Hasan and the officer who came to report the case stated that Yemen was a very corrupted country, and that this rich hotel owner could simply bribe anyone including the judge to get away.

I tried to contact the Syrian Embassy, but they did not respond. I later realized that Syrian authorities were willing to sell any Syrian for money, and we had no protection from our government whatsoever. The extent of corruption reached to the embassies abroad too. Then, this old Japanese businessman Mr. Kinichi, who was staying at the hotel, visited me at the hospital. He repeatedly told me to drop the case and leave Yemen immediately. In the meantime, Hasan began receiving threatening calls and then was offered money to stop helping me. I called my family and told them what had happened.

I lost around twenty pounds in five days. I couldn't eat anything, and was fed through tubes only. Someone at the Syrian Embassy finally told me to accept the hotel owner's offer for settlement, which was ironically reported to me by a police officer. The hotel owner would give me my passport and ten thousand dollars. In return, I'd drop the case and leave the country. The amount of money he offered made me think that the system couldn't be so corrupt after all. Later I learned that raping a virgin relates to honor issues in the Yemeni society, and the rapist's tribe excommunicates him.

Anyway... [*She sighs*] I stayed one night at Hasan's house with his mom, who begged me not to get her son into trouble. Hasan's tribe leader was supposed to help us, but instead he proposed to me! I was exhausted and confused; Hasan was also very upset. He finally told me to return to Syria and promised that he would follow the case on my behalf. On the seventh day after the rape, I left for Syria only to be welcomed by the hotel owner's threatening text messages in my phone. Being back to my home country, I felt stronger and wrote back, "If you want to spend the rest of your life in jail, text me again," and he stopped! My lawyer in Syria convinced me to drop the case and undergo the reconstructive surgery, which I never bothered to.

Dealing with the sexual assault and its aftermath taught me a lot about myself, men, and the value of women in the Middle East. It set me free from worrying about virginity. I consider it to be the final step of being an outcast by the society. Once people in Syria heard of the incident, they asked about virginity reconstruction surgery, but nobody inquired how I was feeling at the time. I even sensed an implied blame of "if you weren't too rebellious maybe this wouldn't have happened!" with a few. I discovered that some people didn't even believe me when I told them, since many girls claimed to be raped instead of admitting that they had sex with their ex-boyfriends before marriage. My family was supportive when I declined to have the surgery. If I was to marry a man with whom I can't share such an important event, I don't want this marriage in the first place.

The following six or seven months after the assault, I mostly stayed at home and didn't do much. I tried to move on with my life, but it was hard. I only went swimming with a friend to release the anger in me. I'd kill myself first before working with Arabs ever again.

On Love and Marriage

I was raised to think that marriage was the natural, unavoidable fate. I really hope to have a relation with someone with whom I can raise a family, which will eventually make my mother happy. She wants to see grandchildren whom she expects to be as pretty as I am!

I can envision myself having children, preferably not more than two. I used to think of marriage as the best possible way to raise kids. I still believe it today; however, I did consider the possibility of having one child on my own. It feels less likely though. I always found adoption to be a really great act of humanity because I believe that parental love is not limited to blood relations. Especially when it is a complete choice, not the last resort, I think of parenthood even more highly. Morally speaking, it is a win-win situation since those who want a child will have one, and this child will have a family.

Marriage is a tricky institution because I can no longer tell whether I want to get married or not. I'm approaching thirty, and my dating experiences haven't necessarily been promising. I can be intimidating as a woman. Hence, sometimes I also worry that a person whom I can trust, marry, and raise a family with may not be around. My biological clock will start ticking in a few years and I'm not in favor of being a single mother. Furthermore, I don't want to have a child after thirty-five because the age gap will be too much.

When I raise my children, I will not teach them religious values. On the contrary, I will try to protect them from their manipulation. I hope to implement in them goodness, love of learning, and questioning things. I want to enroll them in sex-education as soon as possible to avoid any behavioral problems due to repression of their physical or biological needs. But honestly, I have never considered this process of raising children, so I don't really know.

Other Noteworthy Events

By the age of eighteen, I was fed up with all the family conflicts, my mom's putting up with my oldest brother's abuse, and waiting for my father's return. I was unable to take the hypocrisy and injustice any longer. In fact, when I say that, I mean the entire Syrian society, its values, and attitudes, not just those of my own family. All claimed to be one thing but acted otherwise.

One day, I came back from work and found the house upside down. My oldest brother was fighting with my mom again because he wanted money, and he was destroying whatever he put his hands on. As usual, my mother asked me for help, and I told her this was the last time. I went to our relatives' house, and things went terribly bad. By the time I convinced them to come and help my mom, she was friends with my brother again. My brother blamed it all on me as he tried to justify the situation, and called me a slut. He went on explaining that he fought my mom because he wanted her to impose some rules on his shameful sister.

I got so furious both with his lies and with my mother's pretending that they were true! I told my mom in front of others that she deserved him and he deserved her. Then my brother got "offended" and started beating me with all his power. He was much stronger than I was; he hit my stomach and my face. I was helpless.

In comparison to my mother's silence and my younger brothers and relatives' watching me being beaten with no reason, his violence didn't hurt. It broke my heart that all of them saw me nothing more than a rebellious and disrespectful girl. Eventually, my uncle stopped my brother, saying that he needed to reason even if I behaved bad. I was so hurt and confused because I was only trying to liberate my mother from getting abused. That night was the first time I slept outside of my mother's house, the house I used to call home. I realized that I was on my own after that.

I found a job at Petro-Canada as an administrative assistant at the end of 2010. Through this position, I regained my self-confidence and economic independence after the sexual assault. My Canadian hiring manager and his wife became among the best friends I've ever had in life. My Christmas dinner with them in 2010 was the first stage of my healing process in dealing with the rape and my other psychological issues.

Getting accepted to a university in Canada certainly is another milestone in my story. I applied to the World University Service of Canada (WUSC) and filled out two forms: One for my boyfriend at the time and one for myself, but only I was offered the scholarship. It probably was for the better because my Christian Syrian boyfriend's mother had major issues with our relationship. I arrived in Canada in August 2014. WUSC matched my profile and areas of study interest with a university that was willing to accept someone with similar qualifications. WUSC shares many students' profiles with several universities and they have local committees at these universities to place the candidates whom they are interested in sponsoring. When I received the acceptance letter, I got very excited by the idea of studying in Canada so I didn't care which university. I wasn't aware of the differences among universities at the time either.

My Interpretations of Islam and Spirituality: God or My Higher Self?

I was raised to believe in God as a Muslim child, so I developed a very intimate relationship with this untouchable and invisible being in my own way. I believed in a kind and compassionate God, so I had many imaginary conversations, and He always told me that he loved me. For some reason, I thought God was a man. I've never really believed in monotheism but only realized it when I started questioning the entire idea in 2010.

I often thought that the ancient Greek gods might have been real, except that I didn't put much effort into understanding them. My God encouraged me to go into my adventures and believed in my values. In short, I came to observe that the God I believed in was nowhere near the one most Muslims believed in. Hence, I let go of the identification as a Muslim because it made no sense. Plus, people would disagree with my designation due to my liberal values no matter what I tell them.

When I was around five or so, I remember having a dream where the planets in space were showing me respect as if I were very important! When I was a teenager, I had another dream in which I was talking to God, and I was angry at Him but I can't recall how He looked. I was going up to the heaven with some people, and one of them was a bad guy. I got irritated that God couldn't figure him out, but then I was told to chill; the evil guy soon disappeared. After, I looked at the space and wanted to wander around. I'd come later to the heaven but I wasn't sure about the way back. God responded, "Your heart will guide you."

I remember experiencing transcendence as a state where I was so at peace with myself that nothing on earth could affect me. It was a beautiful feeling. That's all that I can remember for now. I was still having some faith when I had these dreams or visions. From a neuroscience perspective, this is understandable considering how I was raised as a child and how I was thinking in relation to God. I still hear this sound in my head that guides me to goodness, but I'm not sure if it is my higher self or God! In short, I've always felt the presence of a spiritual guide in me.

The religion issue kept my mind busy for years. I have always had a genuine curiosity toward philosophy, and I think theology is hardly separable from it. However, at some point, I gave up the religion part. The interpretations of the Quran were unending, and people never seem to agree on certain topics. My major problem was the inconsistencies. For example, if God is all peaceful, friendly, and compassionate, why does the Quran also have statements of hell and punishment? Why are we repeatedly told that if we don't follow God's orders, we'll go to hell and burn there forever?

The other major question I have had relates to the tension or contradiction between free will of the individual and total submission to God. Eventually, I denounced all monotheistic religions, not just Islam. Was there a particular person or text that affected my conclusion on religions? I think Epicureanism, which criticized superstitions and divine intervention. Epicure argued in favor of not having the need for religions or the belief in afterlife. I thought "Wow, he expressed it all so well many centuries ago, even before monotheism." His ideas made sense to me.

I was called Islamophobic by a few female members of a student group on campus, which caused me a lot of emotional pain. I consider myself as the last person to discriminate against someone due to their religious beliefs. I was a believer at some point, so I understand its complications. The girls who argued with me knew little about my background. The values that they tried to attribute to me were very misleading and unjust. They came to Canada from countries where religious extremism hurts women most, and they are preparing to be teachers. Their behavior affected our volunteering team's dynamics negatively. I made an effort to explain myself, and I even offered another meeting for further conversation. However, they chose to remain silent and resentful.

I struggle a lot with seeing the atrocities committed by extremists of any religion, but particularly of Islam. I have to face the fact that people actually value books and beliefs more than a human's life, and they display discriminative compassion!

This incident also showed me how people can get quite aggressive in their responses to different opinions. These two female students even tried to manipulate my position as a chair in our student organization and to stop me from expressing my opinions! I can't change people's minds, they need to go through their own learning journeys, and I shouldn't expect them to know what I know. I should stick to what I value.

For me, denouncing Islam was liberating. I believe my inner strength comes from my DNA and brain. Having good health helps too.

On Beauty and Quality of Life

I strongly dislike cheapness and willful ignorance. For example, I can't stand people who eat bad food and dress cheap, especially when they can afford. I don't favor extravagance. However, one can have elegant places to live and clothes to wear at affordable prices. This requires the touch of loving life and enjoying the little things in it. Possessing too many items, spending money recklessly or wearing only expensive outfits can also be ugly.

Maybe with a few more examples, my views of beauty and ugliness can make more sense: Treating nature with respect and admiration is beautiful. Hence, dumping garbage in nature is a very ugly behavior. Furthermore, people's dealing with their health recklessly is ugly. We don't think twice about trying to stop someone's shouting at a little helpless child, right? I see the same ugliness in someone's treating their own body badly.

Patriarchal values generally cause women to grow hostile to each other and to focus on men as more important beings. A pretty woman is unlikeable because she is considered a threat to other women for she might steal their men. That is one reason why I didn't have many girlfriends. Secondly, having European looks is considered "beautiful" in the Middle East. Most friendships turned out to be temporary relationships. As soon as my female friends find a partner and engage in a relationship, I am discarded. Plus, I didn't share the same values with most of my friends in Syria. Religion was only one of them. Girls mostly considered me a threat as I got most of the attention, and they ended up feeling undesirable. In Syria, family relations and intimate partners are always prioritized over friends.

I have trouble with many adjectives in daily language; ugly and beautiful are maybe the only smooth ones. For example, I prefer not to call myself a feminist or spiritual person as these terms are limited to their traditional stigmas. I would like to be free of all the prejudices that any of these terms might bring on me. I am also aware that this is almost impossible.

Handling Disappointments and Problems in Life

Even as a child, I was always able to see costs and benefits of any incident, and I did my best to reason what's good and bad accordingly. My ability to think analytically doesn't mean that I have a heart of stone. In fact, I experience intense feelings even during my daily interactions with people, but I don't show them. When I am sad or angry about something or someone, I allow myself some time to go through it. I try to understand people's positions even if I feel misjudged. I used to underestimate the impact of the daily events, but now I analyze them carefully.

When my father abandoned us, I thought it was not the end of the world since most of the time he was not there in the first place, which meant that he didn't care enough. When I needed something, my mother was there and she cared; therefore, she was more important and I had to support her. My father announced me as his favorite child but this was a lie because if he truly cared he wouldn't have left me. This type of reasoning has helped me to be less emotional in my reactions and deal with life more effectively.

On the other hand, the incident with my oldest brother's beating me up didn't make any sense considering my mother's response. She had asked for my help so I helped her, and she sided with my brother when I was beaten up in front of everybody. How could she let her only daughter be treated like that? This left me broken because my reasoning failed. My disappointment was so strong because what happened remained a complete dilemma.

Unlike my selfish father, my mother sacrificed her life for us, but I couldn't figure out why she disliked me during those few years. Why did she raise me with liberal values and then let me down when I needed her the most? Not having the answers to these questions made it so difficult to overcome my disappointment.

My relationship with my younger brother who is a refugee in the Netherlands changed for the better (as of January 2018). What he has been going through in the past years must have matured him. In a conversation we had over the phone, he told me that he realized how things were left on my shoulders before 2011 although my family were nice to other people around them except me. I was all by myself to deal with the hardships of life. I couldn't believe what I was hearing from my brother whom I haven't seen in person for several years. His acknowledgment was very touching and powerful because the rest of the family still treat that period of our lives as a black hole and we all act like everything is fine. After the Syrian civil war began in 2011, we, as a family, had to make peace in order to survive. My war with them began earlier and lasted twice as long as the Syrian war today, for about 15 years.

This recent phone conversation with my brother was a confirmation of the path I took despite the lack of support then. I knew that leaving the family was the right thing to do and I wasn't going to play the game of hypocrisy that my circle in Homs were playing. My brother's acknowledgment brought me the hope that actually we can now move forward genuinely as a family, not just on the surface. I suddenly don't feel like an orphan any longer. In all these years, I took decisions by myself despite my family. Although I've always had faith in future, I also had many doubts too because I was all alone on this journey. The "family peace" we made due to the circumstances in Syria might have been a shallow one initially, but now I have the hope that it might turn into something profound. For the first time, I feel like I have a family, not just some people who happen to be biologically related to me and share the same last name. It is such a beautiful feeling.

Getting over troubles in life depends on time, situation, and how I feel and think about these issues. I have made mistakes in life like everyone else, but I don't have any regrets. There are things that I wouldn't repeat, but they are valuable as life experiences. Most of what I did was the best possible thing to do under the circumstances or because I had limited choices or little knowledge. I rarely feel uncomfortable with myself, but when I do, I try to analyze and understand the reasons as I tried to explain.

As Long as I Feel the Value in What I Do

I got my first tattoo which says Allah in Arabic in Syria. While I was going through many difficulties during my early teenage years, I had strong faith in God. Although I grew out of it in time, I still like to keep this tiny tattoo on my finger since it reminds me of where I was and how I ended up here. I got my rose tattoos in Canada. I love roses, and attribute different meanings to them such as Aphrodite, philosophy, and beauty. I love flowers in general: Lavender, daisies, and jasmine of course! It is hard to choose one over another. I guess rose is still my favorite. I like tattoos on people's bodies. They are about little ideas and stories.

I am a very diverse person. There has not been a certain goal, a place or idol for me. I change constantly and I am not one of those people who knows what she really wants to do in life and sticks to a plan. I can't say "I finally have this and now found my soul," stuff like that. As long as there is value in what I am doing, I would be considerably satisfied. I can be many things, a dancer, politician, or lawyer.

Full satisfaction in life doesn't seem possible on this part of the world where we have an insane amount of options. There are always "what if...?" questions that occupy people's minds.

On Canadian Identity and Special People

The first thing I noticed about Canadians is that they want to make clear that they are *not* Americans. This is one thing they keep repeating at every opportunity. But from the perspective of a newcomer or an outsider like myself, they look and act similar. The language is the same; the stores and the structure of the cities are identical.

I observed a similarity to Syrians' constant underlying that they are different from the Arabs or Iraqis or any other neighbors that they have. Their history is more glorious, "ancient this and that," the women are more beautiful and more educated. Syrians have lived in a very mixed, multi-ethnic society for many years peacefully, etcetera. We all know that these things are myths, right? Canadians are also trying to create a similar positive image of themselves. But when I begin having deeper conversations with some of the people I meet or date here, be them Chinese-Canadian or white Protestant Canadian, I see that they are very traditional in many ways. Their families will freak out if they learn that their son is with a Syrian Muslim woman. It doesn't make much difference when I tell them that I am a non-believer; I can still feel their concerns. This whole thing about mosaic-culture is not genuine in Canada, as it is not sincere in Syria either.

Oliver, the Canadian immigration officer who interviewed me in Beirut, was impressed by my story and shared it with his parents Sara and James. He recounted his impressions and feelings about my case with me, and for the first time in my life, someone finally realized how tough things had been on me. I needed the presence of such a person so badly that I almost couldn't believe what I heard from him. I contacted Oliver after arriving in Canada, where he introduced me to his daughter and his parents. We all had lunch together and got along very well.

Later, Sara and James invited me to Thanksgiving and Christmas dinners. I sensed so much love and admiration in them but most importantly, I felt accepted for who I am, something that I have struggled with my entire life. Now I feel a lot of responsibility for meeting their expectations. During the summer of 2016 our relationship was strengthened; they told me that I'm like a second daughter and part of their family. I can't wait to visit them in February [2017].

Sara and James have been married for fifty-five years, so they are the exemplary dream couple for me. They merge the spirit of young teenagers and wisdom of the experienced in their hearts. I came to learn what *they* had to go through in life and managed to build a loving home on their own. I am incredibly fortunate to be part of this family that is made of pure goodness. I can keep talking about them for hours. My relationship with Sara and James is the strongest and the most significant bond that I have.

Not a True Finale

Emilia is larger than life. She is a lover of beauty, knowledge, flowers, dance, and music. Throughout our conversations, she was animated, engaged, and genuine. Maybe she was skillfully performing genuineness, a possibility that I keep at the back of my mind, and it is still fine. Once the trust between us was born and its presence became almost like a third person, she talked about the most serious and difficult topics with a smile or shrug.

Emilia's story doesn't conclude here, because she is still very young and has just opened a new chapter in her life in North America. On the impact of our communication, Emilia wrote: "To be honest, I think I started to look at this journey with you as therapy reflections. So many details and anecdotes that I've shared with you upon your particular questions made me recall things that I thought were forgotten or simply couldn't remember when figured I could. So, thank you for that. Warmly, E."

6

Zizinia's Story
Hopes and Doubts in Unlikely Spaces

Early Memories and Family Celebrations

I was born in Aleppo as the second daughter of the Alhabi family on the New Year's Eve in 1980. I was told that it was a snowy day and nobody bothered to congratulate my parents because I was a girl. However, my father brought red flowers to my mother and they celebrated the New Year at the hospital. I needed special treatment for six months until I looked like a healthy baby of standard size.

My father, an outspoken lawyer, was on the watch list of the Syrian government due to his political views. As a result, although I have no recollections of it at all, I spent six months in London as a baby. When I had my first passport at the age of seventeen, right after high school graduation, I visited London for a second time. The city welcomed me and left a strong impression on me as the symbol of liberation and diversity.

I had a pleasant childhood but outside of my bubble was the single party (Baath) rule which caused a lot of trouble for the non-obedient adults. As a child, I didn't really grasp what was going on but I felt that things were somewhat not right. I was raised as an independent child. All the family stories about me depict me as a hyper, curious, and clever one. I used to try to do everything by myself. I wouldn't let my mother comb my hair, fix breakfast or help me with my homework when I was eight years old, unlike my daughters.

My mother gave birth to my youngest brother when I was eight. I always tried to act like his mom. I wanted to feed him, wash him, change his diapers…. In fact, I begged my mom to leave me alone with him so that I could put him into sleep. As soon as I came back from school, I put him next to me and completed my homework by talking out loud and thinking that he could learn things faster than his age if I kept doing this.

Although we had celebrations of birthdays and the New Year, the *Eid ul-Fitr* after Ramadan stood out for me. This was a time when the whole family gathered at my paternal grandmother's house. Everyone wore new clothes for the Eid, and all children were given some pocket money after we kissed the adults' hands and wished them a holy Eid. We were free to buy whatever we wanted with that money. Unfortunately, we ended up buying junk food, chips, and soda.

The year before my grandmother passed away, we gathered at her place for one last time. I had my first daughter, my cousin brought her two daughters, and my other cousin had three children at the house. They were all kissing our hands and getting their share of the Eid. We made a few comments on how quickly time passed and it was our turn to hand the money for the next generation. However, we noticed a radical change. All the children were saving their money, making their capital grow [*laughter*].

As a child, I identified with Tom Sawyer and Robin Hood who stand by the poor and needy. I always wanted to fix things, do manual work, which was not typical of girls but I could not help it. Maybe I was brought to this world to repair things, be it a broken table leg or injustice against the underprivileged.

What else stands out about the Aleppo where I grew up? The city enjoyed having very different neighborhoods and each one had its own traditions and character. Where we lived was not very special but I can talk about my maternal grandmother's district. Let me introduce her first. She was originally from Hama where the headquarters of Muslim Brotherhood were at the time. She was a very moderate believer but shared the Muslim Brotherhood's hopes of getting rid of the Assad regime. She died in 2000. I still remember her harsh words on how the regime was criminal. "They are just a pack of thieves; they steal our country's resources only for their own benefit," she used to say, may God grant peace on her soul. We visited my grandmother with my aunts and my cousins every Thursday after school was over. We ate Alleponian meals like *mahshi*.[1]

She lived in the Armenian neighborhood although she was a religious Muslim woman. The Christians and Armenians used to come to her house on the Day of Eid and she visited them during their festivities. I remember that her best friend was an old woman whom we called Tante Georgette. She always shouted at us when we came around "Silent, silent!" Yes, my grandmother's neighborhood was definitely different. There were less Muslims than other parts of the city, but it was a happy and harmonious community.

This reminded me of another childhood story about the diversity of Syria and my early introduction to it. One of my father's Assyrian colleagues lived in Tell Tamer [*also Tal Tamr*], a small town in northeastern Syria. My father and I were welcomed in such a warm and friendly way, and I was the only child in this semi-business gathering which made me very proud and happy. However, they spoke a completely different language and I couldn't understand a single word. As we were having tea there, which—by the way— is known as the best tea in Syria, I began to ask them many questions. I also wanted to learn their language! They taught me the first three numbers in Assyrian to satisfy my curiosity, and then wanted to continue their conversation. But I insisted that they taught me more! To this day, I remember how to count from 1 to 10 although I was only nine years old then [*she begins counting in Assyrian*]. I am glad I remembered this special place and people now, and *do* include them in my story.

At an early age, I was concerned about financial matters. One thing was always clear for me, I needed to work and earn some money of my own. My mother didn't like my offers or negotiations with her about this issue, she was not at all a materialistic person. I remember asking my parents many times on different occasions whether they'd pay me in case I completed a certain task such as cleaning the car or the house.

Overall, I was a curious and strong-willed child, and these traits have followed me throughout life. This was a characteristic that I took from my father. He always pushed us to be independent and told me that I could do anything in this world even if that thing seemed impossible. Actually, if someone comments on something as not doable or achievable, I want to give it a try even when it has got nothing to do with me. I am provoked by such comments. Let's say that this table is broken, and nobody knows how to fix it, and they decide to discard it, I must take a close look at it before it goes to recycling. I have this urge to prove that everything is possible and fixable. This is how I survived many challenges in my life. This is also the most important and determining basis of my character.

I went to a private primary school run by the Jesuits in Aleppo, which was the opposite of what the public high schools demanded of the Syrian youth. The school encouraged the curiosity and creativity that I had as a child. I tried to study my sisters' books and I focused especially on science and math. I had glasses and kept breaking them almost every week! However, nobody was upset with me.

I felt more privileged than the rest of my classmates since my teacher was a good friend of my mother and our neighbor. She tolerated my hyperactivity, my eagerness to correct my classmates, and sometimes cutting her off. But I was a hardworking student and got the highest marks, which made up for my behavior. Yes, even at the first grade, I was worried about the final report card, which I think was not very normal.

In fact, one of my earliest memories was about an all day long collective kissing! I was overjoyed about attending school as a four-year-old after begging and crying every single morning at home from September to January. As a New Year's baby, I technically grew one year older in January so I was finally accepted. On my first day in school, I remember kissing all the students in the bus, then all the students in my classroom twice: When I stepped in and when I had to leave for home! It was one of the happiest days of my life.

When I was in fourth grade, I won a nation-wide short story competition, which qualified me for a ten-day-long camp out of Aleppo. The first prize also opened an early door of freedom for me as a ten-year-old Syrian girl. I attended the camp by myself and although I missed the habits of our cozy home, I hid my feeling. It was my first time away from my family and I was very proud.

However, my parents couldn't wait for ten days so they visited me at the camp. I clearly saw the longing in their eyes, they missed me! I loved my freedom and ranking the first in the competition. Honestly, I always loved being in the front lines, under the limelight. Maybe I am more like my paternal grandmother Sama.

What or who turns a child into a free-thinking individual? My answer to this is her parents, her schooling, her neighbors, community, and the parents' friends. In the Christian school that I attended, they had to keep Islam as a subject to teach, but it was monitored by the Sisters. We were also exposed to their teachings at the church and had Christmas celebrations [*Zizinia sent me a photograph of a colorfully decorated classroom, students in casual clothing—no uniforms—and a Santa with a fake cotton beard in the middle*]. This strengthened an understanding of living with others without knowing or calling them as "others" at an early age. We were allowed to ask any question at any time about all religions and minorities, even though we were only children. My school was very different from the public schools for sure where the sameness and obedience were praised.

My Teen Years and Schooling in a Politicized Setting

I didn't think of myself as a magnet for the opposite sex because I was a chubby tomboy teenager with braces. I preferred to play basketball with boys to flirting them. Playing basketball was also a way to lose weight. I remember hiding my body under baggy clothes. I was not interested in wearing skirts or doing my hair. I used to wash my father's car on the street in front of our building, which was not a very girly thing to do. I had close girlfriends though who liked me the way I was. The best friends I made were from the girl scouts' group. There was always room for social activities in my life.

I stole my parents' car when I was fifteen and had a big accident! Miraculously, I was not injured in that trashed car, and my parents didn't get mad at me or react badly. Thanks to their calmness, I managed to regain my confidence in driving. I couldn't wait until I was eighteen, so I kept stealing the new car too! If my daughters were to do what I did then, I might kill them! [*laughter*]

Another very significant time for me was when I graduated high school. My grandmother Sama invited me, my sister, and my cousin to London for three weeks. Flying to London marked my first time on an airplane. Maybe it was the best three weeks of my entire life so far. I remember sneaking out to Trafalgar Square to watch the people after my grandmother went to sleep. I used to see such scenes at the movies and I was finally in them. It was a truly amazing experience.

Going against the Baath Party of Syria meant harassment for life. Although my mother kept quiet about politics; being a lawyer, my father had always been vocal, something I acquired since he was one of my first role models in life. I got myself into major trouble in high school when my younger sister was forced to register to the party. The moment I saw the tears and the fear in her eyes, I went to the principal's office and got involved in a verbal and almost physical confrontation. They called my father. If he were not a lawyer, things could have turned out to be much worse. However, the incident went into my disciplinary records and I was constantly harassed throughout my university years.

The public education is free and required for all children in Syria. However, it is very politically-loaded, militaristic, and monitored by the government. Beginning in primary school, students are taught to describe themselves as the Baath Vanguards. The first year of their secondary school, they are signed up for the Revolutionary Youth Organization. Later in the secondary cycle and at university, they are asked to join the National Union of Syrian Students, all of which are supervised by the Baath Party. At all levels of education in Syria, teachers and faculty are party members without exception. You can imagine how authoritative and insincere the educators' acts and rules can become in such a strict system where one is not given the option to choose or refuse. The Baath Party was the instrument to make all Syrians act in a similar way and follow the leader whatever he decided.

When it was time to choose a department to study, I told my parents that I wanted to become a lawyer like my father but ended up enrolling in the Economics Department at the University of Aleppo.

My father was against my studying law and told me that the atmosphere in general was not for women. He didn't want me to deal with corruption and witness many forms of injustice. He said it would ruin my character because I was always after justice. He pressed hard to change my mind, and I listened to him. However, I didn't do well with the required courses during my first year but passed my law elective successfully.

Almost all the faculty in the Economics Department were old and closely connected to the Baath Party. They had absolute authority over the students. I refused to get enrolled to the Baath as a member. The way they threatened me every year was very humiliating and made me feel that I could never become successful in Syria. One thing I couldn't fix was a personal feud that a professor carried and thus failed me many times. Finally, he was replaced by another professor, and the following term, I passed the course. I already knew then that having a decent career in Syria would be impossible for me and thought of ways to leave the country.

I felt closer to my father while I was growing up. He was the best person ever and an ultimate role model. My mother was a very shy and calm person, and avoided challenges in life. She prefers to be stable and comfortable. But she has a big, generous heart. I took my patience from her and the fact that I don't complain or cry in front of other people. On the other side, my father was an adventurer, sometimes got aggressive, and always struggled against the circumstances of his time, at least, that's what I remember from my youth.

In the past years, they switched roles. My father has become a very calm person and wants to enjoy some stability in life. In contrast, my mother acts more adventurous and she doesn't mind living in Aleppo under very volatile circumstances. They know my involvement in humanitarian aid and discuss it with me and among themselves. My father keeps telling me to be cautious and think twice before I do anything because of my daughters. I am proud that they are my parents and I love them both.

I don't have many memories from my university years, maybe with the exception of the main library. It was a very big space where everybody could study and borrow books. I would spend a full day there without ever feeling bored.

Father Paolo and Zizinia's Grandmother Sama

The gap after my paternal grandmother's passing in 2000 was impossible to fill. She had a unique and non-traditional personality who was in love with life. She always kept the spirit of a teenager despite her wrinkled face. Sharing secrets as well as a cigarette over coffee and getting advice about men and life in general stand out as precious memories of my informal education when I was fifteen. Her words served as an initiation to womanhood only to be rediscovered later.

My grandmother got married at the age of twelve. At that time, it wasn't a problem for the community to let girls marry so early. My grandfather passed away when she was only thirty-six. My uncles and my father did not allow her to marry again, although she was very young. She told me once, "A man will always try to make you a shadow. You are the sun and they are the shadow, believe in yourself." She was really empowering me. I do not see myself someone who needs a man, I never have. I need a partner, not a man, this is how she raised me. It was based on her short-lived experience with marriage, but it was absolutely the most important and useful advice for me throughout my life. I am able to connect with the other sex openly, and I am always a good partner.

These conversations with grandmother boosted my self-confidence and differentiated me from my classmates whom I found superficial at the time. My youngest uncle who later settled in London also encouraged his nieces that we were able to do anything in life regardless of our gender. My daughters are currently missing these extended family connections because of the circumstances in Syria.

I miss my grandmother so much but I'd like to think that she is in a better place because of what has been happening in my country. She would have been in a fragile position due to her age and would refuse to leave the country regardless of how dangerous it might be. She was always very critical of the regime and would curse the corruption and the injustice that were going on in her time. We used to listen to the songs of Fairuz, an amazing singer whose voice delves into your heart.

Some precious informal education took place outside of my family circle as well. Father Paolo was an Italian monk who lived and worked at a historical church near Damascus. He spoke fluent Arabic with a nice sounding accent. He was the first foreigner I met in Syria. I admired his character and how self-sustained he was. I was fifteen years old, and I must have taken him as role model.

For a whole week, he taught us, the girl scouts, how to survive in nature. He made cheese out of the milk from the nearby goats that were grazing freely in the meadows. It was winter time, very cold, and there was no electricity. He was one of those special people whose faces radiated a peaceful inner light that they nurtured so you don't ever want to leave them.

Father Paolo had extensive knowledge of Islam. He was clearly into promoting a religious dialogue between Islam and Christianity. I heard the most progressive interpretations of Islam from him, about women's respectability, talents, and capacities as full individuals. Isn't it ironic yet wonderful for a young girl at that time? My father being an exception, unfortunately, we were exposed to derogatory comments about women in our community. Then, at the girl scouts camp, we met Father Paolo who told us that Islam was the religion which valued females highly, and there were many stories about strong women during Muhammad's time that haven't been promoted today. Idolatrous tribes used to bury girl-babies which the Quran banned immediately when it was revealed to the Prophet because women were valuable. If a woman got divorced or became a widow, a man would ask her hand in a kind, appropriate manner, it was part of the tradition. Women's roles in Islam were different during Muhammad's time. We learned all these not from the imams, but from Father Paolo.

The refined ways that men approached a divorcee or widow in the past have changed negatively. Today, they propose as if they are doing a favor to the woman. A woman is like a tool or an object to be protected and transferred from one man to another, be it the father or the husband. When I hear stories like this sort and get upset, I think of Father Paolo, and his warm smile soothes me. Who knows where he is now, whether he is still alive.[2]

Expressing Myself in a Franciscan-Run Girl Scouts' Space

The seventeenth century philosopher Francis Bacon is considered the father of Empiricism—the reliance on the experience of the senses—over speculation in the pursuit of knowledge. But the senses can be misleading too, can't they? I had seen a lot in the past few years, had my own share of breakdowns and disappointments as a Syrian woman. In fact, I became more religious and spiritual. Many Syrians had to come to terms with their belief systems or practices because of these trying times.

Despite feeling enlightened and mentally revived after the camp where we had the acquaintance of Father Paolo, I came back to Aleppo with a virus. I was immediately hospitalized. After my recovery, I hurried to the girl scouts' local meeting place. It had white empty walls for us to write our feelings, mottos, and messages about our experiences. I wrote my impressions of Father Paolo or maybe the ideas he inspired in me, I can't exactly remember now. The club used to belong to a Franciscan Church which served us secretly. Now they are working under the Baath Party rules and attending there is no longer fun. However, a friend of mine called me in 2012 after seeing my messages on the wall. Maybe one day, I'll take my daughters Celine and Lina to the club, and decipher the sixteen-year-old Zizinia with them.

My daughters are concerned about their displacement and our country from time to time. I consider them my heroes because after what they have been through, they can still enjoy life and become happy. What goes on in their minds is hard to know. Once, Lina arranged a meeting with one of my colleagues through Facebook and made a video about the Syrian cause, expressing her wish for justice and freedom. It took me by surprise but I didn't intervene or criticize her.

On Islam and Religions

I love my religion. I love the version of Islam that I was taught in the family, not in the school. I valued how my parents were filtering the misleading information about Islam which I brought home from outside. I have respect for all humanistic rules that the monotheistic religions keep rotating in the holy books.

I see many connections between Islam and Christianity when I read about them. The main principles that I believe are that there is one God, there is an end to this life, and there is an afterlife. You need to serve other people in ethical and kind ways. This world is not only about you; instead, you are a servant on this earth. But I still believe in the last religion, Islam, and that we need to put all our faith in God with full submission. Unfortunately, we witness many misleading and violent thoughts which are spread by some people who call themselves sheikh. They are not just in Syria but everywhere and I strongly doubt that their religion is the one that God wants us to follow.

I am someone with higher beliefs in our existence, in God, in His books and prophets. One's focus doesn't need to be only on Islam. The full chain of God's letters to humankind composes monotheistic religions. You won't succeed in this world unless you are spiritually strong. This is something that I still can't manage to put into words, but I know how to embrace and practice it in my life. The Quran is the only book which I truly love and am knowledgeable about its chapters and certain passages by heart. Normally, I can't remember a book even on the second day after finishing it, but the Quran is a big exception.

As for the special places which generated spirituality in my soul, I can name two of them. The first one is a place called Taladah near Aleppo where the ruins of Saint Simeon Church can be visited. They say that Saint Simeon, an extreme ascetic who lived in the fifth century, contemplated and connected with God on a small pillar there for thirty-seven years. Every time I go to Taladah, I hear different voices or feel in another world. I close my eyes and I imagine how many people came here and tried the same pathway to have a connection with God. You feel something inside you very, very strong on this spot, I don't know what it is related to, really. This is one feeling that I will never forget when I walk up to this place. You feel magnets in your head. Your eyes get wet but you are not crying. At the same time, you hear people talking around you, but you are not listening to them. There are other voices and other people. It may sound very strange, but it is not an illusion. Every time I visit this area, I experience the same feeling. This is the most affective place for me.

In Istanbul, *Yerebatan* underground cistern where upside-down and moss-covered Medusa's head greets you is another very special place. There are many stories about it. Some people say that they used to keep prisoners there. Then, you have these remains of the statues, two Medusa heads along with dozens of slender Byzantine columns. Water, underground…. I feel myself stronger there, exceptionally connected to the earth, even though there is less oxygen and it is very damp. I feel close to the center of the earth. Oh, I can keep going with *Yerebatan*…. It is a special place.

Spaces of Hopes and Doubts: The U.S., Syria and Turkey

I never have had any doubts about achieving my goals in life. The period after my return from the U.S. in fall 2013 can be considered the only time when I felt losing balance and alienated both to myself and my surroundings, including the loved ones. But I am recovered and determined to continue with the struggles of life, whatever is on the way.

I have been engaged in political and humanitarian aid services since 2013, especially after I learned that my resident permit in Dubai was not renewed. I was told that it was a political decision although I was never provided the reasons. Who knows? I had a valid U.S. visa due to a Syrian friend living in the U.S. who wanted to have her wedding party there. I couldn't make it to the wedding at the time, but my visa remained on my passport with an expiration date in February 2013. When it became clear that I had to leave Dubai, I decided to go to the U.S. The plan was to apply for asylum, and when the paper work is complete, my daughters would join me. My uncle offered financial support, which was very generous and kind.

To have a regular job and a paycheck is extremely valuable for me. I deeply experienced its lack and was negatively affected by it during the nine months that I spent in the U.S. No matter how welcoming my friends were, no matter how distracting the new surrounding and changing scenery of the U.S. was, I missed having a proper job. Volunteer activism, translations, etcetera were not fulfilling enough.

I had times in the U.S. when I confessed to myself that not working was more difficult than being separated from my daughters. I, the hard-working, always the number one girl in the classroom for years, obviously couldn't bear wandering in a foreign country until its government decides to grant asylum one day. If I had a demanding project to work on in the U.S. I could have waited longer, maybe.

My parents were not happy when I announced my decision to leave the asylum application process incomplete and return, but they knew their obstinate daughter. If I made up my mind on something, that's it. The rest need to respect my decision since I am no longer a teenager and I work according to my rules and principles. At least, I do my best.

Maybe it is time to talk about some painful moments regarding my losses and breakdowns during my humanitarian work in Syria in 2014 and on. I only spent ten days with my daughters in Turkey upon my return from the U.S. Whoever the person I had become at the time then told me to go back to Syria and work directly with people in need so I went. I joined my Syrian friends for capacity building projects in a poorly educated community. The locals' lack of trust was immense and could easily ruin our work. They don't trust any woman who looks different. Taking the hijab was equal to having a passport to their hearts and to gain their respect so I did it. It helped me to deliver my messages effectively, or so I hoped.

However, it was also a strange and cruel time for me. Finding the right words to capture my feelings is very hard. I hated myself for obeying a life style that my heart and thoughts did not approve of, but I had to act, perform, despite myself. This created a conflict and hatred in me, which I must have reflected around me without even noticing the cloud of its menace. Can you imagine the radical gaps between the U.S. and Syria that I experienced? I was an open-minded, very independent, and self-sustained woman. I smoke, drive, do my groceries, and I don't need anybody to do things for me. But in this conservative community that I was trying to help people and integrate myself, I soon realized that I was unable to satisfy anyone. After one year, I became similar to them in the way that I dressed or talked, but they still treated me like a foreigner. Plus, I lost trust in people from all directions; politicians, intellectuals, uneducated but naïve nationalists, none of them was able to do anything to save Syria from falling into ruins.

Horrendous incidents took place right in front of my eyes which desta-
bilized my being. I watched a friend die when a rocket hit her car. I got traumatized for one week. Once, as I was sitting in the balcony of the NGO I was
working for in Aleppo, an aircraft dropped bombs and killed four people
right by me. Unfortunately, there were many others but these two affected
me so deeply that I could not function at times and they remain so vividly
in my memory.

After surviving these attacks, my colleagues decided that it was time for
me to leave Syria, to move somewhere else. We decided to open a branch of
the *Space of Hope* in Turkey and I was put in charge of funding and grant
provisions. Both in Syria and Gaziantep, the most important thing for our
NGO is going beyond delivery of food packages. Our team follows up the
mental health of every orphan family, that is, without an adult male, and
assists with community service such as water pumping. By the end of 2016,
the *Space of Hope* team was forced to flee Aleppo, and they are functioning
from the western and northern countryside of Aleppo now. We can communicate daily since most are not in the regime-controlled areas, but the members who risked working in the government-ruled region prefer not to be in
contact with me for security reasons (as of February 22, 2018).

My daughters are here with me in Gaziantep, they speak fluent Turkish,
and are successful in school. My life is smoother and more stable with mostly
overtime work, children, and keeping up with the news of my family members.

On the Path of Maturity

I got engaged at twenty-two and married in 2004. As the days got closer,
I admitted in my heart that he was not the ideal person for me but he was
good enough so I still went ahead. One main reason for marriage was being
able to live abroad and explore my opportunities beyond Syria.

When my father met him for the first time and had a man-to-man talk,
he encouraged Suad to find a job in Dubai and leave Syria for a better future.
Presenting my desire of living abroad as an expectation in our marriage
wouldn't have been appropriate. Well, my father did that for me in a way. I
wish he let me go abroad by myself but even for a progressive man like him,
this was not possible.

Our marriage lasted six years. We got divorced in spring 2010 in Dubai,
and I continued my stay there until February 2013. Because of our daughters'
well-beings, we arrange regular visits and we have managed to stay friends,

which is very important. Suad was living in Adıyaman, 80 miles north east of Gaziantep, but he moved to Gaziantep in March 2017. Since then, my daughters' continuous nagging on trying to get us back together has not been easy on me. They keep delivering his words to me as Suad knows well that they would. He is willing to get back but I am not. I know how I feel about this whole thing and have no intentions to be together as a couple again.

Talking about intimacy in marriage is difficult for me. Intimacy in any relationship is vital, but I have some fluctuating ideas about it. As a human being, everyone misses cuddling or a warm hug.

Today's youth would laugh at our very innocent and intangible form of "falling in love" as we called it then. But that was what we had at the time. In fact, it was normal for a young girl to enter the wedding room without knowing anything about such matters. Thus, I am a proponent of sex education.

Sometimes, one would drag one's self into an unrequited love without disclosing her feelings to the closest friends. I had my share of it too. Other times, you may like a boy, and imagine that feeling to be "love" even if you never get a chance of being alone with him or stealing a kiss or two. All you know is that he is someone beyond a friend, but acting like a friend.

I experienced this feeling once with a boy in my high school. When my father learned about it, he got so mad and asked me not to talk to the boy any longer, which I obeyed. However, this friend stopped me on the street with his dog and threatened me, probably because his ego was hurt. When I told it to my parents, my dad, being the lawyer, got him in jail for three days so that this young man would learn a lesson and not repeat such behavior.

Now that I think about the incident, he was a spoiled son and needed some hard training in life. His family sent him to London after the occurrence. Many years later, we got connected through social media. He became a successful businessman, is married with children. Unbelievably, he expressed his gratitude for my father for the person he has become. Men in our culture are prioritized, but it only does them harm, as simple as that. When I think of my husband who was nine years older than I was, I feel the same resentment against the society. Throughout the marriage, I was the one who assumed almost all the responsibilities, making decisions, and I ended up acting like a man, which was not easy for the feminine inside me. He was not growing up, what could I do?

Sometimes, you feel like you are stuck in the wrong culture where you cannot realize your full potential. I am thinking of gender roles that Syrian society assigns for each person. I hope my daughters will be different and won't suffer from the restrictions that were imposed on my generation.

The red lines of each society differ radically from each other. For example, men-women relationships in Dubai were radically different from Syria, in the sense that they are more relaxed and liberal. Although I don't approve of pre-marital and non-marital relationships, my daughters will make their own decisions in life when it comes to their engagements with the opposite sex. On the other end, I can never survive in Saudi Arabia, for example, because I am against the concept of gender segregation in education and public space. I also can't stand sexism, which grants boys more rights than girls without any logical basis.

Analyzing Myself Through Our Conversations

When I was a child, I associated myself with the animation character Lady Oscar, which needs more probing than we can afford here. She was a crossdresser, warrior, colonel serving the French royal guards to protect the Queen Marie-Antoinette. Lady Oscar was raised as a warrior boy, who developed this special bond toward the servant's son over the years, who was also her playmate. There was an unconsummated love between them.

After the revolution in 2011 began, I started having dreams about Lady Oscar, the heroine of my childhood. The story is set just before the French Revolution of 1789, so I find the timing of this returning dream intriguing. As a child, I was mainly interested in the character's traits. She was elegant, strong, simultaneously a woman and a man. In real life, I was restricted by many customs in the Syrian society as a girl. I couldn't go out by myself at nights, I couldn't travel alone. I was not even allowed to bring friends home without permission while my brothers could enjoy their freedom.

When I was around seven or eight, I used to dream of becoming the President of Syria, to bring salvation and relief for poor people. Of course, as I grew older, I realized the weight of the responsibilities that such as position brings and I forgot about it. A lot of knowledge and a strong personality is required to reach the level of presidency but I think I can still be an advisor if the circumstances were different and if we were to establish a new and uncorrupt government one day.

In my second year of university, I began to work at a kindergarten without my parents' knowledge. I took an immense pleasure out of dealing with children but I also knew that I wanted to do more with my life and this "more" would not be possible in Syria. I needed to go abroad. I wanted to travel.

When I was able to confess that the marriage was a way to reach this goal rather than being a fulfilling enterprise in itself, I decided to raise my daughters differently. I will tell them that if they want to go abroad or travel, they don't need a man. They will have developed enough self-confidence by the time they are of a certain age, with God's willing, so no man's chaperoning will be needed.

My husband arrived in Dubai first and I joined him after a year. In the second week of my arrival to the country, I found a job at an insurance company in August 2004, which I kept until 2013. It wasn't the ideal career maybe, but I was successful in it and learned many things. Besides, my husband was supportive of my career even if it meant sacrificing the family time.

After the divorce, I changed my work and became responsible for Human Resources unit for another insurance company. However, my conscience wouldn't rest. I needed more time to organize humanitarian aid for people in Syria so I went back to my old job and became part-time. I spent many hours connecting people and discussing ways to form alliances for helping Syrians in need.

There is a deep sense of nostalgia about our lives in Syria that my friends and family feel. Did you know that the nickname of Aleppo is Aleppo al Shabaa, Aleppo the White? It is named after the brightness of the marble that was used in the buildings of our once proud metropolis. Being forced out of your country and live below the life standards that you are used to back home or elsewhere is very difficult. My family were members of the famous Aleppo Club or *Club d'Alep* where we gathered for fancy dinners, live music, bridge games, and other special occasions such as the concerts by the maestro Samir Kwefati or Waddah Shibly who also sang at my wedding celebration.

The program at *Club d'Alep* would take start with a selection of Latino tunes, to be followed by Arabic music during the second half. My father would take me to the dance floor as soon as his favorite song "Delila" by Tom Jones began. The Club was part of the life style that defined us, a close community of our family and friends before 2011. I spent some of the happiest moments of my life within those cream-colored walls and decorated tiles, at least, that's how I feel today when I think back and sigh.

In Dubai, we led a pleasant and comfortable life too. We had a live-in nanny from Ethiopia who was like a young sister to me and my daughters loved her a lot. As soon as I can manage, I'd like to have her with us in Turkey, but I don't know how or when. We keep in touch and send each other phone messages and pictures.

After sharing my life story, digging, and exposing some long-buried personal history, I feel lighter now. In fact, I feel more like my old self, Zizinia with her humor, energy, with her music and dancing steps even if the tune is different now. Having a headscarf and leading a life which is governed by my interpretation and practices of Islam does not take away the good old Zizinia at all.[3]

I have also noticed something strange throughout our conversations. I am having a difficult time remembering things that you ask about my personal history, the stuff that I assumed were just sitting in my brain comfortably. But it is not the case. My memory seems to be kind of stuck in the revolution period. Remembering 2011 and on is easier while everything else is harder to reach in my memory. Isn't it bizarre? Having shared my life story with you, I no longer feel fragmented. I remember my old self or maybe I feel more complete now.

7

Leila's Story

My Basic Right to Education
Became Fatal

"This should work," Leila thought. "They can't let me die of hunger, and they know how strong-minded I am." In June 2013, Leila knew that she lost at least fifteen pounds, after she learned the rules and procedure about transferring to a Turkish university. Unlike European countries, the credits from the University of Aleppo would be accepted in Turkey and she could resume taking courses as an engineering student. When the parents were reluctant to let her live in a big and foreign city by herself, she stopped eating.

Leila was a smart, hard-working, and promising student but risking one's life for commuting to regular classes were too much to handle for her parents. When one of their friends' daughter got killed on the same bridge that Leila too was using on her way to the campus in Aleppo, they did not allow Leila to go to university. Leila experienced major depression soon after her parents announced her the news. Then, she found out about the Turkish universities and applied for transfer.

When the plane from Lebanon to Istanbul landed in Sabiha Gökçen Airport in the first week of September 2013, Leila prayed that things go as smooth as possible. Because the direct flights between Syria and Turkey culminated a while ago, she drove to Beirut with her father. He tried to hide his tears by cutting the farewell scene short only to come back and hug her tight one more time. Leila was crying. Life wasn't going to be easy for sure, but her love of Istanbul and her determination to get her degree formed a strong base for facing the unknown challenges of a new life.

Leila's Childhood and Immediate Family

I was born on August 5, 1992, in Deir Ez-Zor as the second daughter of the family. My maternal grandmother announced me the lucky charm of the family because three long-lasting family problems were miraculously resolved on that day! It's an overly-repeated story but I cannot complain. It was carefully crafted since having another daughter before the first one was not even one year old can't be the best news for a Syrian family. I wasn't even blond as she was!

I have always felt supported and encouraged by my family. My parents balanced love among their four children at all times. They made extra effort to ensure a fair treatment within the family. Even when one of us gets hugs or kisses from them, the others would come and ask for the same affection jokingly, "Hey, where is my kiss?" If one parent praises one child for a particular talent or achievement, the other parent would immediately remind the rest of us of our own abilities.

Overall, we get along quite well as siblings. We are two girls and two boys. We used to fight a lot, not any more. I remember the time when my older brother was born because I caused a crisis at home by sitting outside the door for three days, acting very upset that I no longer was the favorite child in the family, and did all kinds of childish things. As a response to it, my father bought me gifts, took pictures together, and told me clearly that my brother's arrival wouldn't change the way that I was loved and cared for.

My brother's arrest in the 2011 protests was my test of love. He was only sixteen. I got so panicked and cried all day. They released him after one day but still…. I understood how much he meant to me. My older sister is in Bahrein with my father. She has a degree in Business Administration and works for L'Oreal. She is likely to start a family soon with my future brother-in-law, a Palestinian-Syrian with Bahraini citizenship! My parents met his parents during their honeymoon decades ago so both parents seem to be content with this match. Just to clarify, it is not an arranged marriage. In fact, we kept it from my father for a while until my sister told us that they got serious. However, there is still a visa issue; her application for Turkish visa was declined. Our visa application to go to Bahrain from Istanbul was also rejected! I won't go into detail but enough to say that we don't know when or where their engagement will be.

My parents couldn't be more different from each other. My father sometimes acts like his father, who was Turkish through his mother. My paternal grandfather was a very respected and disciplined person, known for his strict rules. However, my dad is a funny guy in general. My mother is a sensitive woman. She still regrets and cries over the fact that she beat us up as children, about which we no longer care. She is concerned too much about other people's opinions, and that is troublesome for me. My father doesn't necessarily have the "What would they think if they hear this?" attitude unlike my mother. He is easier to talk to and convince in such matters. I'm his favorite child. I physically look like him and am following his steps in the career path as a future engineer. I am well-organized and have control over my emotions just like him.

I like to explore things by myself whether they are good or bad for me. I have done stuff even when my mother did not approve because I wanted to have the experience. You can imagine my reaction when my mother asks me to behave in certain ways just because of other people, completely ignoring the fact that I lived alone for some time both in Aleppo and Istanbul.

My father is an atheist and my mother is a follower of Islam, at least in her own way. She encourages me to pray and get closer to God, but sometimes she drinks and does other stuff that may be confusing for the outsiders. She was a French teacher so her French is good, but not her English. She says she is too old to acquire a new language and is having hard time in adapting Turkey. Not knowing the language makes her dependent on me and my brothers. Maybe she knows around three hundred words but Turkish is so different from Arabic.

Back in Damascus, what made us different from other families in the neighborhood was the way we lived: We socialized at the balcony and didn't keep our curtains closed all the time. This was considered awkward because we had many conservative neighbors who wore headscarves and never spent leisure time on their balconies. People in Deir Ez-Zor where we lived until 2008 were also more conservative than us. It was a small city, not a fancy one for sure, but all my childhood memories are connected to Deir Ez-Zor. One of the reasons why we moved to Damascus was because my father likes to drink. The stigma about this is very strong there, the daughters of a man who consumes alcohol automatically get a bad reputation regardless of their behavior.

I was sixteen when we moved from Deir Ez-Zor to Damascus. Being a teenager was not fun. I was enrolled in a private high school where most students thought of themselves very highly and acted contemptuously. Because of the region I came from, my accent was different; this caused many students, even some teachers, to make fun of it. To be treated that way as a teenager was difficult to stomach. In response, I decided to focus on my lessons and befriended the hardworking ones.

I was one of those students who studied all the time and had no social life. There weren't many places to socialize and spend time, unlike Istanbul. Besides, girls going out at nights and having fun at dance clubs or bars were not approved of in Syria. I see many young women going out here and it doesn't make them "bad girls."

When I began studying in Aleppo, things didn't change much either. I wasn't a troublemaker, I followed the rules as a dutiful young girl, and I always think twice before I get involved in something or someone. It is my nature, which probably saved me from getting into trouble many times. 2011 was the only year I felt unsafe, and I was arrested once as most of my friends and family. For a nerdy type like me, it was quite an unforgettable experience.

"What the hell you think you're doing, whore?"

May 23, 2012. I planned to attend a protest by the courts in Aleppo with one of my girlfriends. My mother was watching the protests on television and told me, "If you get involved in these, you will get arrested. And if you get arrested, don't bother getting out of the jail because you won't be able to find me. They're going to bring you my obituary."

Her words sound harsh and funny all at once because of the way she said it, but I went to the protest area regardless. Before I did, I gave my friend the phone numbers of my father and sister in case something happened to me. I also wrote a note to my mother, "I can't stand what the Assad regime has been inflicting upon people. I am against him and I can't be silent anymore." I stuck it into my pocket thinking that I would hand it to my friend at some point, but then forgot about it.

The protestors were hoping for the United Nations' observance because whenever the UN team showed up to a protest, Assad would order his officers to act civilized. The courts area was awfully crowded, and before we knew it, we were arrested. I heard one of the officers ordering the use of civilian cars so that that the crowds wouldn't notice the arrest and follow the detainees.

I was detained because of that note to my mother. When a female officer searched my purse, she found it and read it despite my protests. I was in the detention center with another girl and the rest were all men. They took us to a separate room and asked many questions. My fellow detainee calmed me down although the poor thing was beaten badly after her interrogation. She said it was her second time and the police usually didn't beat the first-timers. She was arrested two weeks ago and today was the first time that she was allowed out of the house after her release! I didn't know what to tell her.

She had a long coat, the type that the practicing Muslim women wear along with their headscarf. This style of clothing triggers physical violence because it indicates that the woman is a conservative Sunni. The Assad officers as the representatives of secular Alawites, treat the Sunnis differently from a modern-looking woman with makeup. I belong to the second group although I grew up as Sunni, but I kept it to myself there.

The Assad soldiers are convinced that the Sunni majority is ready to kill them. I have a Christian friend who got arrested three times, and during the first two, the officers kept telling her that the Sunnis were going to kill her with the Assad family. They were very specific too, "The Sunnis are going to throw your bones to the gutters after killing you." The third time, they tortured my friend, who illegally fled Syria immediately after her release. She is now in the U.S. married with a child. Hers was quite a journey: Turkey, Sweden, Qatar, and Switzerland.

I must have been at the detention center with a total of thirty hours, but it felt much longer. I lied about everything the officers asked me. I was only accompanying my friend who didn't want to come to the courts alone for legal advice, and I was content with the Assad regime. Of course, the note in my purse didn't belong to me, "Why would I be so stupid to keep such a note in my pocket if I were a protestor?" They believed me. My stupidity saved me for a change!

I remember the smallest details from my time there. Although I was blindfolded and squatting against the wall, I could tell how clean the floors were. We were at the basement floor of the building so the sounds became louder and louder in comparison to a regular floor with carpets. When the female guardian fell asleep, I began to cry. Soon a male officer came and asked, "Hey, we are trying to sleep here, what do you want?" In response, I simply replied, "I want to go home, I want my parents," and stuff like that. I was allowed to use the restroom when I needed and I had tea at some point. Relatively speaking, my experience wasn't that bad.

But I have this thing, whenever I am stressed out, my nose begins to run. It has always been like that. Not surprisingly, I got the same itches and wanted to take out a tissue from my pocket. When I moved my hands, which were tied at the back while I was squatting, the officer shouted at me immediately, "What the hell you think you're doing, whore?" This was that level of talking, addressing to the female detainees.

Finally, they set us free, me and the girl with the headscarf who was beaten up. Our families were waiting outside and my father later told me that he almost begged the girl's brother not to beat her but be proud of her. There is a saying in Arabic, which is similar to the Turkish "hatırım için" (for my sake) phrase that my father used in his request. I truly hope her brother or other family members didn't hurt her. What she went through was already quite bad.

Overall, despite all the anxiety I had as a detainee, when I look back, I'd claim that I displayed so much power and strength. It was even surprising to myself. Being dragged to the jail in Syria can lead to some really horrible things, especially for a young girl. But I was acting bold and even rude with the officers sometimes. I don't know what possessed me! For example, I remember when they asked me to discard my shoelaces so that I wouldn't kill myself, I did it in a manner that was unacceptable for the officers. The way I positioned my feet was considered disrespectful. The young officer asked me whether I can untie them some other way, and I said no. The same guy called me a couple of times to ask me out after my release so I immediately changed my phone number.

One of the strategies to arrest men in Syria is to go after their women first, be them sisters or wives, and then negotiate with men over them. Once the woman is at the hands of the police, the wanted men rush to the jail to save their sisters or wives from the shame that this experience can bring to the whole family. Women are always used as tools for negotiation.

When I was arrested, my friend who had the phone numbers of my father and sister first called my father. When he didn't reply, she tried my sister's phone. My sister got the news in a hookah café in Damascus, you know *nargile* places like you have here in Istanbul? She just lost it, started crying and all that! As a result, everyone around her learned the news. However, anyone, even the shisha guy who was in charge of checking the coals and serving the customers, could be a spy for the government. We didn't trust anyone in Syria. When he told my sister, "Just give me her name and number, and I promise you she'll be at home tomorrow, I know someone," she realized the possible consequences of her overreaction and left the place immediately. She then called my father, and they went home to share the news with my mom. She later told me how my father hugged my mother tight and held her almost five minutes without saying anything. Finally, my mother asked: "Leila got arrested, right?" She was silent for 45 minutes, no tears, not a single word, her unique state of shock. Then, she began to cry and my sister told me that it was almost relieving to finally see her react to the news somewhat.

As for my older brother's day-long detention story, I can't tell you much because he doesn't talk about it. When he was released, my mother noticed some cigarette burns on his arms but didn't ask questions. He got arrested because his face was shown in one of the videos taken during a demonstration by an informer. He should have covered his face like most protestors did. The Syrian police watch these videos and come after you. Next thing you know, you are in jail! The weird thing is that I had a dream only a few days before he got arrested and I immediately called my mother to warn her about it. She calmed me down by saying that it was just a dream and caused by all the news that I was listening to. I still remember my dream of course because it actually happened. Fortunately, my father had an Alawite friend at a top government position and he helped my brother to get out quickly. Of course, some bribery was involved.

Disappearances and Feeling Guilty About Activism

In August 2013, I joined Ali, a good friend, who was planning to make short videos with the former ISIS members in Raqqa in order to expose how it was like to be an ISIS recruit. He planned to sell the videos to the major news agencies such as Reuters through some contacts in Turkey. Since I wasn't allowed to attend university in Aleppo any longer, I wanted to do something for my country. This was what I could contribute to and this friend was someone whom I had full trust in.

I told my father about Ali's plans and added that I wish to join him on his trip to Turkey and Raqqa. He agreed and shared the news with my sister, but not with my mother because she would never let me go. Ali and I drove across the border and spent one week in Turkey. I told the soldiers on the checkpoints that I didn't have a passport because I didn't want the Free Syrian Army's stamp on it. I was already planning to live in Turkey legally and to resume my studies at some point. Both sides had no problems with my lacking a passport and let me cross the borders. Our journey didn't meet Ali's expectations in terms of business deals or contacts, but it was nice to get away from Syria and explore Turkey a little.

Back in Raqqa, people were so nice; everyone knew everyone. It was just like Deir Ez-Zor where I was born and lived until sixteen. It is a *harem-selamlık* community, where women and men socialize separately. However, because I was working with a male friend, I was able to hang out with his guy friends too, which enabled me to learn their stories in detail. I acted like their sister and they accepted me as such.

In one of those days, Ali's cousin Mohammed disappeared after an explosion by ISIS. It was so hard to believe that such things could happen to the people whom I have known or met in person. They found his smashed camera after the explosion but not his body. His family went to the site and couldn't find a single trace of him. Well, day by day, our lives became like this.

I just remembered another young man whom we interviewed, who got kidnapped by ISIS after the interview. He was studying in Aleppo, but when he got arrested a few times, his family sent him to Egypt to continue his education and stay away from Syria. However, he came back with his girlfriend and they were caught by ISIS in Aleppo. Other people kept getting arrested by the government even after I went back to Damascus. I heard several bad news about people whom I met in Raqqa.

Unfortunately, one day, Ali disappeared too. It has been four years that I haven't heard anything back, who knows what happened to him? I didn't want my end to be like these friends or acquaintances. During that time, my sense of reality got damaged, I think. I was exposed to many stories of people getting killed or kidnapped and they did not feel real after some time. I don't know how else to explain this situation other than a temporary loss of reality.

I had to give up this form of activism after my sister's serious warning over the phone: "You are doing this for our country, I understand your reasoning, but you are not thinking of our own father, who has a history of heart surgery and high blood pressure. I know that he is getting sick because of you. If something happens to him, can you live with this feeling of guilt for the rest of your life?" I have a weakness for my father so when my sister shared some specific symptoms regarding his health, I returned to Damascus. It must be difficult to have daughters in such troubled times.

It could have been quite an experience to join Ali in Aleppo. I wasn't much use in Raqqa, but I was learning the technicalities of videotaping and interviewing people. Locals are less suspicious toward the women reporters or women in general who document the daily life so simply my presence helped.

Friendships and Being an Outsider

I strongly believe that I learn something from every person I meet, but I don't refer to them as special beings or role models. One day, all will go away and they are no longer special to me. Each person who was once in my life taught me a lesson, some of them were harder than others but all contributed to the Leila who I have become today.

However, my father is an exception. He is my hero because he is the one who will always support me no matter what, even if he is in another country. He is in Bahrein now with my sister, but he is still my main support.[1] I guess most people would reply this question like I do, the fathers are the heroes, right?

When did I come to this conclusion about people's leaving my life at some point? Well, after 2011, things changed radically. I used to have this good friend who was part of the nerds' group in my secondary school. I was talking to my friend one day [*after 2011*] and I suggested a group gathering as old friends, but one of the guys ended up saying, "I don't feel like meeting people who are against Assad"! I was so disappointed and thought I should be careful with my words from that day on. I also decided that if someone is not good to me, I won't be nice toward him or her either.

Another example to friends' transiency is the so-called "friends" whom I met in Istanbul when I arrived three years ago. I can't reach any of them today. Syrians care a lot about belonging to a community, there is no denying that. I was thinking one day if I get married who would come to my wedding? Having a community has always been important for me.

The biggest pressure or the challenge of living in Turkey is actually being a Syrian. People realize that I am a foreigner the moment I open my mouth, but the thing is they don't know and cannot guess that I am from Syria. Once it is revealed, you should see their faces. I have experienced that moment too many times already, now I almost turned it into a game. I chat for a while with people before I tell them that I am Syrian and get a pleasure out of their responses.

Leila's First Day in Istanbul, Followed by More Relaxed Ones

It is hard to forget the day I left home. I first drove my younger brother to school and he acted so cool about our separation. However, I was crying the whole time while driving. He didn't want me to come all the way to the school entrance, probably felt embarrassed by his crying sister. I hugged him and drove back home, still crying. I stayed in the car while waiting for my father to come down, and waved to my mother from the car. I had already said goodbye to her and it would be even harder to repeat the scene if I went up again.

The car belonged to my sister, and she normally didn't want me to drive it, claiming that I lacked the experience. However, when my father came down and I moved to change my seat, he gestured me to keep the driver's seat. It was very sweet of him to do so and I drove all the way to Beirut, which is about 90 miles. I was paying attention to the road and not crying this time. Doing this favor for me was his smart and quick way to ease my pain of separation and to distract me with driving. We checked into a hotel, then spent some hours walking in Beirut and woke up at around 3 a.m. so that I could catch my flight on time.

My arrival in Turkey was not the most welcoming one. The daughter of my mother's friend promised to meet me at the airport but didn't show up. Being the cautious, organized person, I had insisted on getting their address in case something happened but my friend dismissed it. What was worse is that my cell phone didn't work in Turkey. I had been to their house before so at least I knew that I had to cross to the European side of Istanbul, which required several transfers and taking a taxi.

I ran into another Syrian who offered me a ride-share and assured me that the taxi fare won't cost more than ten dollars per person. He got off first and I continued, but the swindler at the wheel kept demanding more money than what the meter showed. Our argument got serious when I began throwing my stuff to stop the taxi. One passerby intervened when he saw me crying and shouting at the driver in Arabic. I said "No Turkish" to him and continued crying. This gentle person talked to the driver, came back, handed me a tissue, and offered his cell phone to me so that I could make another call to the family with whom I'd be staying.

When I finally made it to their house, the mother was not welcoming, which aggravated my anxiety. She probably had some psychological problems because the rest of the family were treating me nicely, but not her; and I still have no idea why. She was such good friends with my mother back in Syria. She left us the key to their empty house in Damascus and would call us to check on it from time to time. If the Syrian soldiers noticed that the house was empty, they would come and simply occupy it. That's why my father used to go there to act like it was our house to guard this family's property when they had moved to Turkey three years before I did. After a few days in Istanbul, my father told me on the phone to leave the house because of the woman's attitude.

Once I rented a place thanks to the daughter of the same family, and settled down, my younger brother joined me. However, due to his lack of managing or sharing household responsibilities, he ended up causing more stress for me than being a supportive companion. My mother arrived three months later to rescue us, and assumed her maternal roles. When my other brother got accepted to Bilgi University as a civil engineering student, I somewhat felt more intact.

However, I am not necessarily happy with the dutiful daughter roles that I am expected to fulfill once I walk into our house in Fındıkzade. Some of these gender roles are so hard to change. I can tell you one story regarding my paternal grandmother. She would set the table and we were all about to eat. When I am hungry, I become a completely different person, I get so grumpy. Anyway, as I was ready to place a scoop from the pot on my plate, she would stop me and say, "Serve your brother first!" and it would drive me crazy. We still joke about it today as siblings, but this "privileging boys thing" is in the culture and very annoying.

The Most Powerful Tool: Education

My first memories of school go back as early as I was three years old. I recall having bad feelings about being in school. Both my grandmothers failed in child-sitting so my mother had to bring me to her work place, which happened to be a school.

My mother's friend was a kindergarten teacher in the same building. She was very sweet. I remember her taking me to the restroom and feeding me with small sandwiches. In Syria, when you are six years old, you can go to primary school and attend classes as a guest, we call them "listener" student. When I became one, the teacher, known to be very short-tempered, treated me so nicely that her memory also stood out for me. I was an eager and hard-working student and always got the highest marks even though I was only a listener and thus was not responsible for official grades.

Education plays such an important role in my life. The most depressing time I have ever had was when I was deprived of higher education due to the war. Education gives everyone more opportunities in life. I have to admit that I respect people who are educated more than the ones who are not. Similarly, I expect people treat me more respectfully when they learn that I am an educated person.

However, it doesn't mean that the ones who lack formal education know less. In fact, some of them may read more and be more knowledgeable than the educated ones. Nevertheless, in general, I believe that it is imperative to receive the best education one can have access to. Education can be a powerful tool in a variety of situations. One of my reasons to study hard during the middle-school was to please my parents. I wanted them to be proud of me and forget their marital problems through my success.

Today, my biggest worry is related to my degree. I get panicked sometimes with the fear of failing or not doing good enough. I cannot leave Turkey now but my plan is to go to Europe or Canada legally at the first opportunity that I will be granted, and build a career there.

In Syria, we need to pass the "baccalaureate exam" in order to receive our secondary-school diploma. This exam takes place on the same day and at the same time across the country. Approximately two weeks before the exam day, each student gets an ID card with a number to be able to take the exam. It is a nation-wide standardized test which also designates the department that you can attend if you proceed to university. This test was a major source of anxiety for all Syrian students; now, we have other anxieties!

When I was in the seventh grade, I wanted to be a telecommunication engineer, but I didn't study hard enough in my last two years of high school. Because those private high school students were making fun of not just my accent but also my study habits. I wanted to show them that I can be "fun" too so I stopped studying at the expense of not becoming a telecommunication engineer. I needed to perform better to qualify for it, but my score was sufficient for the environmental engineering among some other options. My father told me that environmental engineering was not so different from studying economy, you make decisions to build roads and other things. Then, my cousin who works for the Red Crescent in Syria told me that we can't realize many projects in Syria because we lack environmental engineers, which highly affected my career decision. Initially, I didn't like it much but now I really do.

Aside from the formal education I have received so far, there are some life lessons that I learned which will accompany me for the rest of my life. The first one is not to trust anyone but yourself. Secondly, do not ask for help or depend on others if you want something so strongly, because people will tell you that they are going to help but in reality, they won't. People love talking and making promises but when it comes to actuality, they pull out. I also knew early in life that friends leave but not the family so I never became one of those teenagers who would die for their friends. At some point, friends go to their own ways but the family remain and support you.

Istanbul as the Greatest Irony of My Life and Some Memories

My first visit to Istanbul was with my father in 2009 when I was seventeen. I was fascinated by the city and I told him that I wanted to live in Istanbul one day, and he replied, "Inshallah (God's willing), your dream will come true." At the time, we didn't even need a visa for crossing the borders, Erdoğan and Assad were like brothers. Nobody could imagine the horrible chaos ahead of us in Syria.

After I had to move here to continue my education and heal myself from severe depression, I was faced with some challenges that were beyond me. When I get sad or angry due to these difficulties, I remind myself that this city was my dream place, and I prayed for living here one day. Some moments in daily life catch me off-guard and suddenly fill me with gratitude. For example, while I am looking out of the window on a bus and I find myself murmuring, "I'm so grateful to be here. It still is a great joy."

Other "happiest moments" in my life? Getting high marks or becoming very successful in school, which was not the reason but the bridge for happiness. I noticed how my performance made my parents happy at a time when they were not joyful otherwise. Secondly, moving to Damascus. I knew that the city offered many opportunities unlike Deir Ez-Zor, so it made me and the whole family happy. My first year in Damascus was amazing. Taking courses at the British Council improved my English immensely. I began playing guitar too. The only problem was the contemptuous attitude of the students and teachers in my high school, which I mentioned earlier.

I have to say that the people of Damascus have an attitude. It is the capital and we are all taught in school that it is the oldest city in the world etc. However, as most of us would claim, the best years of one's life are usually the university years, right? Since Aleppo was the city where I began studying and lived by myself for the first time, I love Aleppo more than Damascus. I find it cleaner, I like the architecture and the food better, and people in Aleppo are more generous. Plus, they don't ask condescending questions to the people who come from other cities unlike the locals in Damascus. When my family moved to Damascus from Deir Ez-Zor, I was exposed to very ignorant and insulting questions as if they lived on another planet.

My worst memory relates to my cousin who passed away on July 26, 2012. I heard that he got shot in Syria, but I postponed calling and sharing my feelings with him. I thought he'd get better and *then* we would talk. When I learned about his death, I felt awful because I couldn't say goodbye to him. [*Leila cries*] The way I was informed about it added more to the shock. When I got connected to Facebook, one person wrote me, "I am sorry for your loss," and I wrote back, "Who died?" and he had to tell me, of course. It was one of the worst moments in my life.

On Relationships

I don't feel comfortable talking about my crashes or other experiences with the opposite sex. However, I can tell you that I am very skillful at creating a sister-like bond between me and any guy with whom I don't want to develop a special relation. It is harder for me to become good friends with girls.

I remember the first boy I liked. I was at eleventh grade and we were classmates. I shared it with my mother and sister, but not with him! Simply because it is not appropriate for a girl to tell a boy that she likes him; it is the other way around, you know? At least, that was how I felt at the time.

In order to get to know a person closely, I believe you need to spend a lot of quality time with him. This goes true for friendships as well. But let's say with a boyfriend, it is important to go out for dinners and see how he behaves during those dates. Moreover, traveling together can teach you a lot about your companion. There was a proverb that I can't remember exactly, but it was something like "You need to do three things before you claim to know a person really well." One was to travel, the second one was to eat or drink together, and I have no clue about the third one, sorry.

My current boyfriend is Greek guy who is a professional guitarist and plays with various bands. We have known each other for a while but taking our acquaintance to a different level took a while. I think it is getting serious because he cancelled his plans of moving to Greece from Istanbul. I told my mother about him, but not disclosed much. She didn't seem to mind his nationality or our religious differences; however, you can never know with mothers. If the possibility of marriage arises, then the responses might change. I don't think of marriage because it seems like a very complicated thing. Plus, I feel like one needs a stable job, a stable life first. Getting married would make me feel old![2]

I think Turkish men are similar to Syrian men since we share the same culture, socialization, and geography. They too are jealous and they attempt to rationalize their control mechanism with love, claiming that they are acting jealous because of the strength of love and thus restricting their girlfriends. I observe such behavior in my circle and was shocked to witness several times how some girls complied with it. I haven't even let my parents monitor me in all these years when I was out so who are you to inquire into my whereabouts?

"Truly, where there is hardship there is also ease": On Islam and Being a Muslim

We have a large extended family and everyone respects the other when it comes to Islam since we all have our own interpretations of it. I go to clubs at night, I drink from time to time, but I also pray. In terms of family traditions, we always celebrate our birthdays and New Year's Eve in addition to the *Eid al-Adha* and *Eid ul-Fitr*.

We all pay attention to our eating habits during Ramadan. This means that we don't eat in public or in front of the people who are fasting. If there are practicing guests in our house, we wait until the sunset and eat with the ones who are breaking their fast. I also enjoy celebrating the end of Ramadan. We have a rich breakfast to share once the fasting month is over.

Next to my mirror at home, I posted a line from the Quran, "Fa Inna Ma-al 'usri Yusra" (Truly, where there is hardship, there is also ease.) This line from *Sura Al-Inshirah* gives me hope and instills the belief in me that after some challenges in life, relief will follow with the help of Allah. I'm not that "Muslim-Muslim," but I try. Oh, what do I mean by that? Well, I think a real Muslim is someone who is always close to God, not only when she needs God. I am aware that I pray more in difficult times or before the exams. But I had some special and inexplicable moments too.

Once, I was praying and suddenly I began to cry. I kept asking myself "Why am I crying?" As soon as I was done praying, my aunt's husband came and announced that my father had a heart attack. It was a strange moment which filled me with rebellion, "God, why did you do this to me, I was just getting closer to you?" Well, things like that.... I used to see or hear people crying while praying, but it never happened to me before that day.

We have a saying in Arabic and it translates like "if you want something so much it is going to happen one day but only if it is indeed good for you in the long run, which you, as a simple human being with limited vision, cannot know whether it is good for you or not. We then say, "God will let it happen if it is *khayr*." If it's not, God won't let it happen to you even if you feel very upset for the time being. This is something we hear and use repeatedly in our conversations in Syria, and I believe in it. Believing in *khayr* is also comforting but who is to say it is not true? However, I have to confess that when bad things happened to me, such as getting into jail, I caught myself thinking that maybe they occurred because I was not close to God as I should have been.

The appearance apart, I'd consider myself a good Muslim and someone who is devoted to God in her own way, because I don't hurt anyone and I treat people kindly. I may not be fasting or praying five times a day, but I sometimes read passages from the Quran, talk to God, and recite some prayers. There are a lot of people, who fast or dress conservatively, but they may not be good Muslims when you look inside their hearts.

Happy Ends?

Although I am the rational type who doesn't like to show emotions, I daydream. It is the only way to lift me up at the moment. I dream of becoming a successful professional and exceling in my job. I dream of a long happy weekend breakfast with my family as we used to have in Syria. I dream of having my own house in a safe place where I can host my family and friends. I also dream a lot about traveling around the world which requires not just money but the right passport. I have always wanted to travel the world and explore new food and cities, but today, I can't travel anywhere. However, one day I will get the life that I want.

I sometimes get the nagging question of "what if I can't?" I try to get rid of it and focus on my goals instead, but it is not easy. This feeling of being stuck in a muddy pool of annoying problems bars me from even enjoying a book. After reading a few paragraphs, these thoughts rush into my brain.

As a teenager, I used to believe in happy endings. I had no doubts about achieving my goals but I am no longer so sure of that, not after 2011. When I wasn't allowed to attend university due to the security issues in particular, I became very depressed. My family couldn't come up with an alternative plan so I made the research and decided to transfer to Istanbul. This meant however, moving to a new city with no friends or family to support me, I had to face everything by myself. Sometimes I get panicked even with the idea of getting as depressed again. It was awful. If I am depressed or hungry, I can't think clearly so I do my best to avoid both situations.

My younger brother's arrival in Istanbul made things even worse because I found myself in the role of his mother, which I refused to perform. Then my mother finally arrived, burdening me with more responsibilities because she lost her circle of friends and extended family by moving to Istanbul. Thus, I had to socialize with her, show her around, and be her interpreter, just to give some examples. All these things made me stronger.

My parents raised me with the conviction that I was a very strong person and I can do whatever I set my mind to. It is in accordance with my sign Leo as well so I still hope to hold on to this belief. At moments of desperation, I cry first, and then I talk to my family, they are always good at supporting me emotionally.

I have self-addressed notes of encouragement posted around the house. As I said, I am afraid of getting depressed and giving it all up. I focus hard on keeping my hopes alive somewhere inside me because I don't want to leave things incomplete. I need to get my university diploma.

We are in a limbo in Turkey. When the military coup attempt happened in July 2016, the uncertainty of our situation was unbearable. Similarly, just before the constitutional referendum to approve proposed amendments [16 April 2017], I remember worrying, "What is going to happen to the Syrians if Erdoğan loses?"

One of our acquaintances was arrested soon after the coup attempt because she was teaching at one of Fethullah Gülen schools.[3] After spending a month in prison, it became clear that she had no connection to the foundation or the movement, she was given the option to leave Turkey immediately as a "favor." Well, as a Syrian, you can either go to Malaysia, Sudan or back to your country. As a single woman, guess what did she decide? She told my mother that to be killed in one's home country sounded better than to be imprisoned in a foreign country or start from scratch in a faraway place such as Malaysia. She went back to Aleppo. What would *you* decide? Living in constant vagueness and insecurity has been the major cause of depression for most Syrians. Can we move on to the other question?

Is there one emotion that makes me feel deeply alive? Yes, it's love, and it doesn't matter where love pours from, friends, family, partner.... Feeling loved makes me feel alive and happy too. However, if you ask me what the most important thing is at the moment, I wouldn't say love. Graduation from university is my top priority and I know I'll be very happy on that day. Moving to Istanbul was the greatest challenge of my life; beginning a program at a new university, trying to communicate with people in a foreign country, learning a new language.... All these are done for sake of completing my education. I remind this to myself every single day.[4]

Miscellaneous and Serious

I like many neighborhoods in Istanbul, but Kadıköy and Taksim are my favorites. Anywhere by the sea is fine with me, I enjoy being near the water. I feel comfortable with nightlife in Istanbul. Clubbing women in Syria are automatically considered bitches, men would come and ask how much you'd charge for spending the night with them! You need to have a brother, cousin, male friend, or fiancé to accompany you. It doesn't happen here.

Speaking of men, I'd like to say a few things regarding my younger brother about whom I complained earlier. He is actually a very talented violinist. He has been playing for the Istanbul Municipality City Orchestra and stood out from early on so much so that his instructor called my parents and asked them to consider conservatory instead of a regular university. He insisted that my brother should become professional with the talent he has. [*Leila takes out her phone, we watch a video where her brother is playing in the orchestra during one of the national holidays in Turkey. I point to the irony since the concert was to celebrate a national day. She laughs and tells me that nobody knows that he is Syrian. He speaks Turkish very fluently with no accent.*]

Sexual harassment is always an issue for women. In Istanbul, I still experience catcalls like I used to in Syria, but at least here men are afraid of the officers unlike Syria. In Taksim, when men bothered me a few times, I told them if they didn't stop, I'd go to police immediately and they left me alone. I think it is important that women talk openly about these issues, and that's why I support #MeToo movement. However, when my mother learned that I shared something on Facebook, she woke me up at midnight, and I had to go to university the next day, and told me to erase what I posted. I was pissed so refused it, and she threatened me to report it to my father, the same old tactic. A similar thing had happened when I participated in the Pride Walk last year in Taksim, Istanbul. My mother was worried that people who saw me there or read about it on FB would think that I was lesbian. I went ahead and marched with the LGBTQ community. I don't care what others would think, I know myself, and I will march against any injustice.

With the limited leisure time that I have, I practice a dance called Balfolk, which originated in Europe five hundred years ago. If you google "Balfolk Istanbul" or visit Facebook Balfolk Istanbul, you can see our group and how we dance. It is easy and so much fun! Aside from this, I teach Turkish to Syrian children and give Arabic lessons to anyone who is willing to learn. I teach English to my friends and my roommates. Finally, I volunteer as an interpreter during the food aid package distribution to Syrian families by the municipalities and NGOs. I am well connected to the community of volunteers here.

When you asked me about my favorites, I can hardly remember any names, sorry. I enjoy watching *Game of Thrones* and my favorite song is "Dance me to the End of Love" by Leonard Cohen.

I am not sure whether my replies were satisfactory, but thanks to this interview process, I remembered many good memories, not only the bad stuff. Sometimes we need to consider both the good and the bad things that happened to us. You reminded me of the good things that caused happiness once in my life along with some unpleasant memories which almost made me cry a few times, like my cousin's death. But overall, I experienced both happiness and sorrow. I also remembered many things that I thought I had forgotten long ago. Above all, I see myself very differently than in the past. In other words, I didn't know that I was so strong. It is a valuable realization and a surprise!

8

Sara's Story
De-Bordering of My Life So Far

May 1, 1991, is the day I was born in Latakia. I am the eldest of four siblings. I was followed by another sister and two brothers. My name, Sara, is both religious and global, plus easily pronounced. It was a smart choice for my parents who, at the time, hoped to move to Russia to make a better life, a plan which wasn't realized. I think my father's aunt was the only person in our whole family who emigrated and that was some decades ago. The rest are provincials who seem to be content with where they live and don't have plans to leave the country no matter what happens.

My sister Samara's name is made up, and my brothers have clearly Muslim names. My parents favored their daughters for a change, but only in naming! I pass smoothly any place I travel. People in Greece expect Syrian women to wear the hijab, but I have no idea how or why they have this stereotype. A woman like me with a nose stud, jeans, and one-side-shaven brown hair doesn't look Syrian to them. We can talk about this later as we proceed to my traveling to Greece and the type of attitudes that I have been dealing with since I left Latakia in December 2015.

I was raised by very conservative Alawite parents, which was not a very pleasant experience to say the least. I can't consider them educated although my father had two years of college training. I hardly have any recollections or anything that is worth citing for this story until I was 15–16 years old, really. I don't remember much. Maybe I don't want to remember. There was quite a bit of physical abuse, beatings, insults, close supervision and whatnot. It was pretty much the same boring home-to-school commute with lots of restrictions and rules imposed by my father, who was a sheikh. My mother was always on his side out of fear or for whatever reason, so that affected our relationship negatively. I was not a social child and I took it for granted after a while. The thing was, my parents were not social either. My mother never liked mingling with the neighbors, never attended their regular gatherings, so I guess it was normal that I turned out to be asocial too. We never had birthday parties or other celebrations except the two religious ones each year.

There was always tension and shouting going on in our house, and I am sure that the neighbors in our building heard everything. However, we were not the only ones fighting since I used to hear our neighbors' shouting and bickering as well. The building was not soundproof and everybody pried into each other's lives. I hated it because I suffered from it. All the women checked on other families' daughters: when they came home, what they wore, who they talked to on the street, and all kinds of things that were none of their business. My mother did that too, but at least she chose not to hang out with neighbors and thus couldn't gossip about other people's daughters. Nevertheless, her awareness of the prying eyes and gossiping caused us to pay the price.

I had the same best friend from kindergarten until the end of secondary school. We were always together in the same classroom for 12 years! Her mother was our teacher when I was in fifth grade. Our mothers knew each other. She didn't come to our house because my mom didn't want us to have guests, but I went to their flat many times. When I turned 16 or so, I became less religious and acquired many new ideas that were shaping a new self inside me. When I shared my secrets and my opinions about LGBTQ individuals, my friend stopped talking to me and told others, "I don't know what is happening with Sara. She has become a totally different person. Her mind is filled with evil ideas," and so on. Then she began to act distant. Gradually she talked to me less and we spent less time together. When we began university, she dropped me altogether. We never had a fight or a major argument; we simply drifted apart because of this widened gap in our mentalities. We no longer talk to each other today. What was irritating for me was that she was always the same. If I left her for 10 years and came back, I bet she would talk and act exactly the same. I'm the opposite. I change all the time and I remain open to new ideas and adventures.

In such a provincial and religious community, how can one create ways to have fun as a teenager or university student? I did crazy things just to get some taste of freedom. When I say "crazy" I know it's all relative, and compared to what many girls in other cultures do as "crazy," mine can be considered very naïve. I've never told this to anyone before, but I skipped classes several times and I traveled to nearby cities to visit friends during the day when my parents thought I was in school.

If I had to lie, I lied, but I am so bad in making up stuff. It is better for me to keep quiet. Any average person can catch my lies; you don't need to be a genius to see through my stories. Since I arrived in Athens and gained my freedom, lying has become even more challenging because I am out of practice. I don't need to lie to anyone!

Regarding your question about belonging or feeling close to a community.... Well, I don't like this idea of "belonging" in the first place. In the end, I am a human being and I can adapt to any community. Since I was a child, I have wanted to become a translator and to help people, which I can now define in adult terms as "to become involved in humanitarian aid." Another clear plan is to work for justice. This has been very crucial for me. I will do everything in my power to defend LGBTQ and women's rights, not just in the Middle East but across the world. There are still many places on this planet where women don't have equal rights. In the end, I'm Syrian, but I don't like to stress that. I repeat, I am a human being. I feel I belong to many communities and as soon as I find myself in one group, I automatically begin to stand against other groups or don't want to belong to them, right? There are many people in this world who need help and a chance to express their rights, and I'll be there with them.

One of my major principles in life is to disregard categories. I don't want anyone to categorize my personality, my body or my mind. I don't like this at all. As evidence of this, I've never become a member of a political party although I'm a leftie. Even at university, I didn't get involved in politics or other activities. True, I was inevitably enrolled in the Baath Party, but that was a given in Syria and not worth the fight. I want to be free; I want to say whatever, whenever. Memberships may impose restrictions.

More on Family, Failed Bonding and My Early Years

My first memory is my mother's taking me to primary school. I was very excited and my mother told me later that, unlike most children, I didn't make a fuss or cry. I think I went to kindergarten for one year before that but I really have no recollection whatsoever. You asked me about the games I played or other stuff that I did as a child, but I am sorry, I can't remember much from my childhood. My life began when I was 15. Until then, I was a relatively calm girl and always ranked number one in school.

Oh, you just made me remember two events that I realize only now had left some strong impressions on me! The first one was the day when our ground floor flat was completely flooded and we lost everything. I must have been 6 or 7. I remember running to a car with my siblings. Then my mom took us to our neighbor's house for some relief and shelter. I was very sad because, only a few weeks before the rain, my father had brought us some beautiful toys and we lost them all. None of our paternal relatives took us in during that time so we ended up going to my mother's village, which tells you something about my father's relations with his extended family and how it affected us. We stayed at my mother's relatives' home until my father found another place to rent.

Another incident was an earthquake after which we spent the whole night outside. There were no fatalities or major damage, but I remember feeling terrified and wondering what would have happened to us if our house had collapsed.

An unforgettable day, as in any girl's life, was the day of my first period, of course! I must have been 13 [she laughs]. I was watching TV one night and I felt something, some strange pain in my abdomen area. I knew something was wrong. I went to the bathroom and saw blood on my underpants. I was very scared and went directly to my mother, who was asleep. She came with me to the bathroom with a sanitary napkin, showed me how to use it, and said, "Congratulations, my daughter, now you're a woman!" I was like, "What the hell? I've got blood in my private parts, strange cramps, and my mother is happy about all this?" The next day, my aunt and grandmother came home. They were also very happy and complimented me by saying "Now you're a woman." [she laughs again] That's how I felt during my first period.

I was a practicing Muslim child until 15 or so. My father's position as a sheikh made him a respected religious figure in the local community although he was also very strict. Syrian Alawites are not necessarily liberals, especially if they live in rural areas. Maybe the women don't wear the hijab, but it doesn't make them any less conservative than the ones who do. Making assumptions about how we dress and live our lives is very misleading. Even in Syria, I met people who were confused about this and oversimplified things by thinking, "Oh, she is from Latakia with no hijab, so she or her family must be liberal."

Neither of my parents showed affection, and I didn't have grandparents who might have spoiled me. However, I have heard only good things about my grandparents, so they clearly left a respectable and honest name behind. Not that I care about such things.... I don't believe in the standard family structure, but, still, it is good to know that they had a good reputation, as far as I can tell from people's reactions when I mention them.

My relationship with my mother is difficult. To begin with, I never understood why she didn't take the side of her daughters, being a woman herself. Instead, she regularly egged my father on when he was punishing me. When I was around 16, she sensed the danger of my becoming a different type of woman. She couldn't express or understand what was going on, but she had to do something about it. She was afraid that my behavior would affect my younger siblings, so, in her mind, I needed to be put on track. She kept me at home, hit me, and made up lies about me so my father ended up beating me as a way to keep me in line. He was away from home all day, so he never actually witnessed what we did. He was "informed" only by my mother and he chose to believe her, not me.

My mother deserved an Oscar for her performance when it came to playing with our emotions! The day after she beat me, she would cry and say things like, "It's all for your own benefit. I am your mother, after all; why would I ever want to hurt you?" blah blah…. The simple truth was that she didn't know how to deal with me. It became clear to her that I wasn't going to be the dutiful daughter who would excel in housework and learn to be a good future wife and mother under her shadow. She was prepared to execute her plan or nothing, so she acted very imbalanced and inexperienced in dealing with a different daughter like myself!

I'm kind of close to my sister, Samara, and carry her pendant, which has our common initial S, as a constant reminder of her. I am not very close to my brothers. In fact, let me just say it straight: in my family, I have been the only one against the Assad regime which automatically set me apart. However, if your parents and siblings are his admirers, what can you do? You need to share the same household with them, so would you argue and create tension every single day?

My Two Mentors

When I was 15, I had a teacher who changed my life. Let's call him "Mr. Spiritual"! He was a patient and charismatic man who took the time to introduce me to new ideas and worlds through books and conversations. During this period, I began to question Islam and religion in general. I realized that I was a unique individual and nobody had the right to impose their lifestyle or to prevent me from seeing the real me inside. Before I met him, I pretty much lived in a small, dark box without much knowledge about the rest of the world. Once my mind expanded with new and fascinating ideas, I denounced religion and stopped practicing. I would call myself agnostic today but things may change in time.

The joy of volunteer work came through Mr. Spiritual as well. He gathered a large team of volunteers from the community, and on Fridays, our "Sunday" in Syria, he played music for children and organized activities such as singing, mural painting and drawing. I helped him with these gatherings, making sure that everyone got involved and all had a chance to express themselves.

My teacher urged me to save the books I read and value them for what they offered me. He told me to accept differences and not to judge people by their appearance. He valued listening over talking. I remember his reminding me many times, "Sara, you need to listen more than talk. If you want to grow up, you need to listen to people, and be very careful with your words. Once they are out, you cannot take them back."

This wonderful Mr. Spiritual gave me an unforgettable advice: "Sara, I see this fire in you. Please keep it alive: be yourself. The secret of success in life is feeding this enthusiasm in your heart. The fire burning in each human being is very important, so I don't want to see you reaching your thirties and becoming cold because you couldn't keep this fire going. You would be like a robot. Nevertheless, if you lose a fight for whatever reason, remember that it doesn't mean you lose the war. There is always hope to rekindle the fire." Whenever I feel down, disappointed, and hopeless, I remember his words and try to be and feel the way he imagined me to be.

During those years, I also had questions regarding my sexual orientation. Through the Internet and Facebook, I discovered a new language on gender roles and learned how other women from different cities saw themselves. I had had feelings for a girlfriend before, but I never dared disclose them. Now that I have come out as bisexual and know more about these things, I can go back in time and analyze my feelings which then had no name. Last year, I even contacted that girl who was special for me then, and we had a nice exchange about the past. She had come out earlier and told me during our online conversations that she had known about my tendencies but did not want to force me to come to terms with them. Now I can recognize them and I am very glad that I do. I have become familiar with the terminology and debates that have been going on in LGBTQ circles both inside and outside of Syria, but mostly in Syria. I came out a year ago in my own network, with the exception of my family, of course. For them, comprehending and dealing with this new reality will be very difficult.

There was another person who helped shape my personality. Let's call him "Mr. Hairless" since he was bald! We met in a café in Latakia through a conversation about music. I asked the waiter about the music they were playing and he pointed at Mr. Hairless. He was nine years older, and he immediately understood that I was quite different from most Syrian women he had met. He could have convinced me to have a relationship if he had wanted. Instead, he said I was too young and he wouldn't get involved with a girl for amusement, but only if he intended to get married. I owe him a lot for introducing me to European movies, different books, and music in various genres. Our long conversations had to be secret, yet his family knew that we had spent hours together. They even assumed that I would be his future bride. We had a major argument just before I left Syria, about which I don't want to go into details here. I still feel indebted to him for the doors he opened for me and the world views he offered me.

My Education, Jobs and Dreams in Syria

Because of my parents, I studied pharmacy instead of English language and literature, which was what I *really* wanted to study at the time. Once I understood that their choice had to be accepted no matter what I wanted, I convinced myself to complete it as soon as possible and continue with my life. It takes five years to get the degree and I finished it on time. The first years were a nightmare. I hated it! The only regret I have in this life is lacking the courage and self-confidence to stand up against my parents' pressure on this. I didn't feel strong enough then because I knew that if I had chosen the English program, they would have threatened me with money and told me to be on my own. In time, things got better. I began to see the benefits of a degree in pharmacy, and also met nice people at the department, which eased my anxiety. Overall, compared to the high school, which was within walking distance to our home, university meant more freedom for me. I also felt that my identity was formed during the university years.

I have had three main dreams and I am still working on them: to learn several languages and become a professional interpreter, to become independent and stand on my own feet, and to get involved in humanitarian work. As soon as I can enroll in a prestigious course to become an interpreter, I will proceed more firmly on my path. I am still looking for an internationally recognized institution.

After I graduated, I worked as a pharmacist for two years in Latakia. It was a good experience and when I actually got to practice it in real life, I began to enjoy it. However, my parents demanded my earnings, so I had no money to fulfill one of my passions: dancing. I managed to enroll in a contemporary dance course with an excellent instructor, and in order to afford it, I began working at a restaurant during my lunch breaks, washing dishes. As soon as the instructor learned about this through a casual conversation, he stopped taking money. He was an idealist and considered spreading love of dancing his mission. I attended his classes only for 3–4 months before he left, but I want to continue dancing at the first opportunity.

After Syria: What Istanbul Meant Then,
What Athens Offered Me at First

Sometimes I look in the mirror and ask myself in an affectionate tone: "Hey, Sara, how on earth did you overcome all these incidents in the past 18 months? You were not even allowed to go to another city by yourself, and now you are in Athens, employed by an international NGO, after crossing the Aegean on a packed boat from Izmir."

I was stronger than I thought. Yes, I took the most common route among refugees but I am legal and that makes life relatively convenient. Otherwise, I couldn't be hired by an NGO to begin with. In a month [*as of December 2, 2017*], I will be moving to my own flat. If I were illegal, there is no way that the landlord would let me rent her place. Now I live with other NGO staff in a shared space. I am aware that having one's own flat means more responsibilities and paying monthly bills, but I am looking forward to it. I remember the time when I worked late hours in Latakia only because I dreaded going back home. Now, it is completely different. I want to go back to a place where I feel comfortable and enjoy a space with my own rules and taste. That's what home means for the moment.

My six months in Turkey were not pleasant, to say the least. The day of my arrival was unforgettable though because it marked my first day of freedom as a young woman: December 21, 2015! I lit my first cigarette on the street and blew it in the air with an overwhelming feeling of joy. That cigarette was my statement of freedom because, for a woman, smoking on the street is not accepted in Syria. At a New Year's celebration in Taksim, I met a Syrian man named Youssef who pretty much took me under his wing without my realizing it at first. He was an interior designer who had found a job in a prestigious company in Istanbul. Being in Turkey as a young and single Syrian woman makes you an easy target, but with him as a roommate, I probably avoided most of the possible dangers. I found a job at a private hospital and worked for a month as their marketing representative, but I left because they were not very honest. It was also implied that I should ignore customers' harassment over phone marketing. Nevertheless, my first month in Istanbul was beyond my imagination. Coming from the small town of Latakia to Istanbul…. How can I express my excitement and shock? I was on Istiklal Street (Taksim) on my first day, and I was staring at the street musicians, hundreds of bars, live music, a constant flow of people from all directions, many young girls and women smoking outside…. I had never seen anything like that in my life. Okay, I have to admit that the happiest time of my life—after the time I spent with Mr. Spiritual—was these first couple of weeks in Istanbul.

However, by the end of my six months in Istanbul, I was so depressed and frustrated by the Turkish people that I couldn't get out of bed. I couldn't lift a finger; in fact, I wanted to die. Youssef encouraged me to leave Turkey and take control of my life in a better place. I couldn't leave the house for three months, not even to go to the market next door. It was a dark period of my life, so when people ask how long I lived in Turkey, my real answer is [*the first*] three months. The last three months shouldn't be considered "living." I came to a point where I told myself to choose between suicide or a possibly fatal ferry journey across the Mediterranean.

I can't tell you the extent of exploitation that was going on from all sides in Istanbul. My initial excitement at being out of Syria faded quickly after harassment and labor exploitation, so I made an arrangement with a smuggler for one of the most dangerous boat journeys. I couldn't afford any better option. I paid only 500 Euros. I took a bus from Istanbul to Izmir, and then a boat to Greece.

The worst time of my life so far was when I was homeless in Athens for six months. I simply wasn't thinking when I jumped on that boat. I had no money other than the fare for the smuggler, which I handed over once I landed in Greece. I didn't know anyone; I had nobody to call and ask for help. I was truly alone. The first week, I slept on the streets, park benches, or wherever. Then you meet people one way or another, and they offer you a couch to sleep on temporarily, and then you move to someone else's home. Some people gave me money or food to survive. Weeks and months pass until one day you cross paths with someone who has some authority or holds a position in an NGO. I am not ashamed of having been homeless and I wish I could tell you more, but the problem is my memory. I am not hiding anything on purpose, but I have major gaps about those six months. I have the feeling that they were horrible in the real meaning of the word. Isn't that weird? I can't remember much but I know that it was an awful time to go through.

On one of those days, someone whose house I was staying at introduced me to a female psychologist who worked for an NGO helping the LGBTQ refugee community. After our initial meeting, as soon as she learned that I had no papers, she arranged a lawyer for my asylum application. Both of them spent several hours with me for the interview preparation. I needed to pass this interview and the female therapist was with me throughout the whole process, thanks to her NGO. No, she was not volunteering. It was part of the service that the NGO was offering to LGBTQ asylum seekers. She was with me during the interview to protect me and to be a witness to the questions. I was lucky because the interviewer was also a psychologist and told me at the end of the interview that I needed to see a psychiatrist [*we both laugh*]. Those interviewers are really experienced, so they knew that I was not lying.

Once the paperwork was sorted out and I got access to health benefits in Athens, I began to see a therapist on a regular basis. I was also looking for something to contribute to, to keep myself busy—anything would do, including volunteering, which eventually led me to my current paid job in an international NGO.[1]

My Story of Finding a Job in Athens

I heard of a Syrian immigrant activist who has been something of a celebrity for more than two decades in the left-wing, anarchist neighborhood of Athens called Exarchia. I began volunteering at his team as a translator in a makeshift pharmacy in one of the squats that he was in charge of. That is where I became friends with someone from an international medical organization who introduced me to his supervisor. She expressed interest in including me in her team because of my dynamism and the way I was running nonstop among the patients, the office, and the pharmacy. However, in order to be hired, they needed official papers and my diploma. In one week, I received an original, notarized copy of my diploma from my friend in Istanbul to whom I entrusted all my important documents. Because I took the ferry from Turkey to Greece, I couldn't risk bringing anything important with me. Having survived that episode, I was able to see my university diploma once again thanks to the postal service.

My interview went well, and I got a real job, which was indeed the realization of a longtime dream, that is, engaging in the humanitarian aid field. The supervisor, who left the organization a few months ago, was extremely supportive, I owe her that. She even helped me edit my resume and told me to change my English proficiency from B-1 to B-2, which is upper intermediate. Before she left, she told one of our colleagues, "I found a piece of God when I worked with Sara," something so powerful that I'll never forget.

My role in the NGO is to coordinate communication and education campaigns on different themes in order to support our medical activities. They include promotion of the medical services and hygiene, and information on themes linked to maternal health, and malnutrition. I also deal with emergency projects if necessary. Like many other people in the field, what really upsets me is the way that the Greek government is dealing with the refugee crisis. We know that the government was given a lot of money from several sources, not just the European Union's budget, but nobody knows for sure where exactly the money is going. I came across many cases where injured or sick people were not treated in a timely manner so they lost an organ, or their health was damaged permanently. All because of negligence! Anyone who repeatedly witnesses such cases can't help getting very upset.

I am a realistic person with dreams. I can pursue them under whatever circumstances life brings along. I don't like the way people use the word "hope" because of its religious connotation for me. You need to work hard, not just hope! [*She pulls up her sweater to show me a tattoo inscribed on her inner arm in black Arabic letters* دوام الحال من المحال *which means "Nothing is forever."*] I chose this part of my body because I wanted to see it every day! I still have very difficult days in Athens and the number of problems I encounter both at work and in my personal life is beyond my imagination. I take a deep breath and a long look at my tattoo.

Listening to My Body and Mind

Until the asylum process took place and I received an ID, I had felt confused and disoriented for six months. Not only that, but also, I was filled with fear mainly because I thought I was losing my memory and didn't know what to do about it. I have always been proud of my good memory, not shopping-list or phone-number memorization type of memory, but memory for details of events and people before my arrival in Greece. I hope it never happens to anyone, but forgetting memories of people, places, loved ones, including the faces or basic information about my immediate family and my feelings toward them, was very, very weird and scary. Then the psychologist explained to me that these were part of what he referred to as post-traumatic stress disorder. He told me that it was my system's defense mechanism and that my body was protecting my health by blocking or hiding certain memories and information. In fact, he assured me that I hadn't lost them; they were temporarily hidden, and when I become stable again, they will come back. I also learned after a few more sessions with him that I was considered a red-line level patient or something like that—I forget the exact term he used for diagnosis—but it meant that I was physically and mentally in danger.

I have suffered from chronic sleep disorder for the past 8 or 9 years, long before I left Latakia. As a pharmacist, I had access to many pills to experiment in Syria but I was very cautious. To give you one example: Gabapentin is a prescription medicine used for neuropathic pains, but it is also used as a drug. You can empty the powder out of the capsule, burn it, and inhale it.

Gabapentin leads to quick addiction but I chose not to become an addict. I had already tried several sleeping pills in Syria, and each time, I found myself needing higher doses, simply because my body got used to them quickly. I stopped taking pills altogether and suffered sleepless nights instead. In Istanbul, someone introduced me to weed and I was pleased to discover that it actually helped me sleep. When I was living with my parents, I couldn't smoke anything at home, let alone weed, but it is my sleeping aid now.

I smoke pot every evening. Unlike tobacco, marihuana is not addictive since it disappears from your system after 48 hours. I hope to quit smoking one day and stick to marihuana only as a sleeping aid. I don't use it to change my mood and I have never smoked outside of my room, definitely not at parties for socializing. In any case, addiction to herbs is better than sleeping pills that doctors prescribe. I know that nicotine is addictive because after three hours, I want to smoke again. If I don't smoke, I get really mad so I know that it is physically addictive. But dependency on weed is psychological. I hope one day I can quit smoking. In fact, I am against any kind of smoking for youngsters under 18. I haven't done it myself. I think they shouldn't have sex either. Their bodies are still developing. But that's another topic, I guess. Sorry for the diversion.

I studied and personally experienced the side effects of sleeping pills and weed. I know now that my body deals better with weed's side effects than any lab-made pills. Some of those prescriptions can cause suicidal tendencies; you can read the warnings written in the tiniest letters in their prospectus. I have tried to kill myself three times in the past 10 years so I don't need to add any risks of suicide due to some sleeping pills. I had diagnosed my depression and insomnia before the therapists in Athens did, and I have been trying to deal with them by listening to the reactions of my own body and mind as best as I can.

Whenever I smoke pot, I wake up relaxed and fresh the next day. However, sometimes, when my mind is fully occupied with major and seemingly unsolvable problems, I need to smoke more and even then, I sometimes get up in the middle of the night. Last week, I smoked a lot and still couldn't sleep properly, maybe because of the pain in my leg [*Sara fell down a few days before our meeting and had a limp*] and many other problems.... I'm really tired. [*I ask if she wants to take a break but she declines. We wave at the waitress and ask for our second cups of coffee*].

Look, I know that I'm not addicted to weed because a few weeks ago I spent the weekend at a girlfriend's house up in the mountains. She has five children and a very kind husband. Although I didn't smoke there, I slept better than usual because of the relaxing environment, fresh air, the company of a nice family, a festive mood, etc. I was hosted at her house after a difficult week at work, and I spent one full day sleeping. There are several ways that your body takes care of itself, but you need to listen to it carefully.

Finding Ways to Cope

As a health promoter, I deal every day with so many people whose stories are very difficult to listen to. These accounts stay with you and can take you to a dark place even when work hours are over. That is why I see a psychologist every week, which is included in my insurance. Even when we talk about problems or challenging days at work, many other things come up. We communicate in English. He is very professional—no, he's not the one who diagnosed PTSD, but this one is also good.

Although I believe in the benefits of psychologists, we need to remember that they are specialists like other professionals. I mean, if you come across a bad doctor who can't diagnose your illness, then you need to see another one who can provide details and explain what to do about it step by step. It is the same with therapists. One can really help you and save your mental health, then you are referred to another who doesn't know what to do with you, and ends up making you much worse actually. I see mental health treatment just like physical health. In fact, almost all the people I work with in Athens have regular visits to therapists because of the nature of our jobs.

I've got my own ways of dealing with the pain that hangs on from work. I guess everybody has a survival tactic. I take long showers, cook, and clean the house even when I can't do anything else such as dancing or working out. I realized that when I am cleaning the house, I can be all by myself. For centuries, housework must have been a good excuse for women to create their own time to meditate even when they were trapped at home. Nobody can say anything to a woman when this "me" time is disguised as household tasks, right? Maybe it is a subconscious thing, but I discovered it by chance after I spent many hours cooking. I couldn't eat everything I cooked of course, and I ended up feeding other people. However, I felt very relaxed after the cooking was over. The same thing happens with cleaning, too. Recently, I read an online article "12 Rules of Taking Care of Yourself," and you can also check it out and pick the ones that work for you.

Spending time with close friends is one of the cheapest and best ways to tend to your mental being. I miss being with my friends in Syria, sharing a cup of coffee, a meal, or a smoke with them. One of my best friends, in fact the first male friend I had, was a classmate from university. His name is Hasan and we have been really good friends since 2009, which is a long time for me. He is a very kind and smart human being. Now that I think about it, all my good friends are far away and it is one of my biggest problems. Hasan got stuck in Syria; he can't leave. Because of our busy lives we can't always be in touch. Besides, each time we talk, one of us ends up crying. Being separated from one's best friends by unforeseen forces is very painful, so maybe it is better not to be in regular contact. Working hard, at least for me, is one way to deal with the pain of separation.

Another very good friend lives in Germany now. She is a few years older than I am, and a mother with two children. I don't call her much because I know that she is busy with her kids and also working. But when I had bad times, she helped me and I felt very safe when I was with her. If only I could, I would sleep in the comfort and security of her arms. After a long day in Athens, just to make myself feel better, I think about her and imagine myself hugging her. I am glad I already told her these things.

On Intimacy and Marriage

Relationships between men and women can be experienced in so many different ways. In Syria, as you also know from Turkey, intimacy with the opposite sex is limited and not approved at all outside of marriage. Even if there were no deadly conflict in my country, just this stupid attitude and the pressure of traditional marriage would be enough reason for me to leave Syria. I never wanted to become one of those women who gets married, has a couple of babies, does housework, and lives the rest of her life controlled by her husband and in-laws.

I have had many relationships. Some involved sex, and some did not. Some of them were initially friendships, but in time, we added sex to it. Sometimes, I just had sex without any love or friendship, and other times, it was possible to have all three, which sounds pretty intense. I don't like the word "boyfriend" to refer to the special person who has been in my life for some time now. He is not in Greece with me, but I know that he is more than just a boyfriend so I began to call him "my fiancé." He is my love, but in English, to call someone "lover" sounds a bit weird to my ears. We have several problems but if we can resolve them, we might actually be together. I don't know.

Having a long-distance relationship is very difficult. I am already dealing with many issues and not having him physically here in Athens causes me extra frustration. We sometimes spend hours on the phone explaining things to each other. If he were with me, however, maybe just holding hands, a hug, or one loving look when I get home would be worth more than hours of conversation. Anyway, that's all I can say about him or our relationship for now.

I am not against marriage itself, but the way it is handled and experienced in Syria. It is just a fucking paper that you both sign in front of an authority. For me, marriage is about love, understanding, and expressing your desire to live with that person. Getting married has never been among my dreams or plans in life. However, I would like to have a good partner whom I can count on; who truly loves me, that is, loves my way of thinking, my personality, and lifestyle; and supports me under all circumstances. I don't care about signing the papers, but meeting someone whom I can live with for the rest of my life is very difficult.

When it comes to children, I never wanted to have my own biological children. It is a principle thing. I don't know whether my mind will change in ten years or not, but at present, I feel strongly about adoption. If I have a good partner, who is psychologically and financially stable and strong, I would suggest adopting children. I am thinking of adopting two children, one from Syria and one from Africa.

Viewing My Country from Afar

Although the world sees the Syrian conflict as a new phenomenon since 2011, it is actually the result of long-term repression, favoritism, and corruption going back several decades. I recently read the novel *1984*, and couldn't believe how similar the situation in Syria was in terms of Big Brother watching you all the time, the fear of criticism, and the horrible education system. I had heard of *1984* before, but it was banned in Syria, not surprisingly. I analyze the political events in Syria from a global perspective; that is, there is a dictator who has been violating human rights as many similar figures have been doing for centuries across the world. Basic human rights are not too complicated.

If you want to have a peaceful, steady, and developed country, two sectors need to be of high quality: justice and education. Let me talk about the very, very problematic education system in Syria. We need a complete revolution, which is still one of my dreams because I have several ideas about how to make it happen. Educating teachers is the first step. They need to be open-minded and very well trained both in their fields and in pedagogy. Only certain subjects are favored in Syria; arts, sports, or sex education are not among them. In fact, we don't have sex education but it is very crucial to include in the curriculum. I am also in favor of removing religion and add more electives that can trigger students' talents in various areas.

Children are amazing beings. If you just spend some hours observing kindergarten and primary school kids you will know what I mean, yet, their teachers don't give a shit about their talents and intelligence. What is worse is that they shut these children up if they try to express themselves. We only memorize things which are useless outside of the school building, and exams are based on spurting these useless things out on the paper; really, it is simply a copy-paste system.

If you are very passionate and talented in math, what are your options in Syria? I know such people who become math teachers and that is end of their story. How can you excel in a society where only medicine, law, and engineering programs are respected?

I wish I had the opportunity to learn how to draw. I have a very rich imagination and fantasy world. I feel that I can only capture it through drawing, not through music or dancing although music makes my life very meaningful. I would love to be a graffiti artist for example, but, instead, I have been collecting pictures and illustrations from the Internet or social media such as Facebook or Instagram. Sometimes I see a picture or caricature and say, "Aha! This image really expresses my imagination or my ideas!" but I don't know how to draw. Another skill that I want to learn is swimming. I grew up in a Mediterranean city on the seashore but we had no swimming classes. You see what I mean by a revolution in education?

I don't believe in borders. I believe that any human being should be able to move as he/she sees fit. If she likes skiing and cool weather, let her go to Scandinavia. However, in the real world, I happened to be born in Syria and my mobility depends on my passport. Is it fair? I know I will have to live in Greece for some years until I receive a new passport and become a more "acceptable" human being because of the stupid paper work. I will do my best to utilize my time here and improve my skills in the humanitarian aid area.

Spirituality and Controlling One's Life

In regard to spirituality and whether I have control of my life.... Well, as you know, I am an atheist, or rather an agnostic, but this doesn't mean that I am not spiritual. I disconnect this wonderful word from religion. Anyone who triggers special emotions in me, empowers me by guidance and wisdom, or makes me a better person contributes to my spirituality and is a spiritual person. Spirituality relates to inexplicable feelings, so even now I am having a difficult time defining the word. Remember I chose the nickname "Mr. Spiritual" for that special teacher I had in secondary school? My feelings for him were profound and unique.

Spirituality can be connected to one's inner strength as well. Some people have a calm confidence radiating from them. They know what they want in life, and they are well aware of their abilities and also limitations. There is no confusion in their minds or in their ideas when they talk. Those people are admirable and I hope to become one of them some day.

I believe nothing is impossible and, if we are determined, we can create the circumstances needed to achieve our dreams. Therefore, we can have control over our lives but only to a certain extent. We all constantly make decisions and choose one thing over another. This is the control we have, and we need to take responsibility for all these decisions. However, I am not alone on this planet, and there are too many things and people that are beyond my control and somewhat affect my decisions. In other words, they too have influence over my life, so I need to adjust myself to the changing environment and laws, adapt my life to these events while taking decisions.

I stand behind many of my conscious decisions, and I don't give a shit if they were wrong or right. I'll give you one example: I decided to leave Syria and came to Istanbul in 2015. It was also my decision to leave Turkey without much preparation. Maybe if I had decided to learn Turkish and get involved more in Turkish society, my life would have been very different. If I had left Syria earlier than December 2015, I'd probably be in Germany today, not in Greece. But my decisions then were shaped by circumstances such as my financial situation. I wanted to do a variety of things but I wasn't able to because of money. In the end, I made the decision to come to Greece, but I can control my life only to a certain extent.

The Way I See My Future

My plans reflect my main fears. I want to have a stable life, which means a steady income, a house, some savings in case I lose my job, as well as acceptance of who I am, of my past and present. Because I experienced homelessness and joblessness, those two things have become my nightmares. I don't want to work like civil servants at a 9 to 5 job. I want to establish my own business, to become indispensable because of the originality of my ideas and service. In today's world, innovation is so important; you have to come up with unique ideas that nobody thought of before. In this way, even if you work at a private company where competition is high and there are always younger people applying, they still cannot lay you off.

As soon as I have the financial means and a European passport, I want to travel the world. I learn so much from new cultures, countries, and novel ways of thinking. Traveling makes humans more open, and we accept others more easily. When we meet new people, they may look or sound very strange at first, but after talking to them, we discover many things and thus become richer beings. I have to confess that Islamophobia was one of my problems before I came to Athens and began this job. Now, I deal with many practicing Muslims, women refugees in particular, and I realize that they are not as narrow-minded or problematic as I thought they would be.

The thing I pay the most attention to in life is not hurting others. When I say "hurt," I include any kind of injury, not just physical. Think of a child. I consider many children to be victims of their parents because their minds are controlled by the education and the societal rules that their parents choose for them. To me, it is a form of invisible violence if a child's unique personality and talents are suppressed.

On the one hand, I believe in the immense potential of human beings, that we can realize anything we imagine. I also remind myself that everything in this world is temporary and this includes all the difficulties and problems that hit us in life. I feel better when I look at my tattoo and remember "nothing is forever."

In general, I feel sad because many people are suffering and no one cares about them. I already told you the difficulties that I have faced so far. If we humans continue to live the way we do now, I feel that this planet will soon explode or throw us out [*she laughs*]. We absolutely need to respect nature and accept each other as we are in order to live harmoniously. I favor freedom of movement for all and I repeat, I hate borders.

9

Bidaa's Story
"Read, read and read..."

Starring My Centennial Grandmother and Mom, the Boss: A Large and Strong Family

I was born in Aleppo on February 1, 1984. We are a family of seven siblings, our oldest is 34 and youngest is 17 years old. We have university degrees in different disciplines. One of my brothers and I are lawyers. One sister works at a bank, another one earned a degree in English Literature. She got married in Dubai and is now in Sweden with her husband. They left in 2012, and my sister already acquired Swedish citizenship. Another sister is a computer engineer. Our youngest sister wants to be a gynecologist, but she is learning German to adapt her new country as soon as possible. You see, education is extremely important for my family. Without hesitation, I'd count the day I graduated from university as the happiest time of my life.

My mother is a homemaker and my father is a retired officer. If only she had formal education, my mother could have been a prominent figure in Syria. She is my role model as a smart, friendly, and organized woman. Before the war broke out, we all lived together and shared everything including our salaries. Our friends envied this special family bond, and joked about us being like a small kingdom: My parents as the King and the Queen, we the children are the soldiers of their castle. We take decisions together and as children, we respect our parents dearly.

We are very thankful to God that my father reached retirement one year before the war. He went to Mecca to perform Hajj and began a different life with his family. We used to have midnight picnics in the mountains of Aleppo when he was finished with his shift on Fridays. The city was safe and lively then, and we never felt distressed about driving from one city to another at night time. In Athens, I don't feel safe after dark. There can be drunk men

147

or people sleeping on the streets who have no fear from the police unlike pre-war Syria.

My maternal grandmother lived until 96, my paternal grandmother was 120 when she died. I know it is hard to believe but it is true. Until her last days, she was able to pray five times a day and prepare her own food. She lived in a village near Aleppo and led a healthy life. I can give you some tips about her longevity. She rarely ate meat except the chicken breast, which was rare. Her diet was made up of eggs, yogurt, olive oil, honey, and Arabic butter, which she made at home from cow's milk. I still remember the lovely smell of the butter filling the kitchen whenever she opened the jar. It is called *samneh* or clarified butter in English. She ate a lot of dates too.

My paternal grandmother had a lively and humorous personality. She always had some solution for ailments. If she had sleeping problem, she would eat yogurt with some drops of lemon juice in it and tell us how nicely she fell into sleep after that [*Bidaa mimics her and we both laugh*]. As an antidote to menstrual cramps, she would advise eating a teaspoonful cumin and in less than 15 minutes, they are gone. I tried it many times and it works! Olive oil is good for everything, not just in cooking or with *zaatar* at breakfast. If you warm the oil and massage it to the aching or stiff parts of your body, especially your neck or stomach, you will feel much better. Cover the painful part with a clean cloth or even a plastic bag works for a couple of hours and you will thank me for the result.

Remember that the Quran mentions certain fruits such as olive, grapes, fig, dates, and pomegranates.... These are not coincidental. They are considered superfoods today and very beneficial for our bodies in many ways. Take figs, for example, they are best for constipation, right? You soak a few overnight and eat them the first thing in the morning. Voila! People can look up the rich nutrients in the other ones if they want, but we can lead a healthy life just by consuming these Quranic fruits, honey, and other halal food which are not mentioned by name but clearly categorized. I used to tease my grandmother saying that she looked like a model whereas many women around her were overweight. In return, she would joke back with me: "Bidaa, why are you still not married? Probably all the men who will ask for your hand will be lined up once you open your law office." She was a character for sure!

My grandmother's attitude toward life and people in general is also worth discussing. If someone was upset, cried, or complained, she simply showed her the door and told straightforwardly: "Please come back when you are done with these issues, I don't want to see tears or hear complaints in my household, until then, take care!" [*Bidaa laughs again.*]

My best friend's name is Waed and we met in high school. I consider her my family although our very first encounter may sound more like a love story! I remember the exact moment when I saw her near the library and wished that she became my best friend. Later, she told me the same. We studied law together although she is a few years older than I am. She chose to work for the government, I opted for the private sector. However, we worked in the same neighborhood, our offices were near to each other, which allowed us to keep a close daily contact. One of our rituals was to go to the same small corner bistro to have falafel, which we called "it doesn't count!" The nickname we gave to the pre-dinner falafel session meant that it was only an appetizer and an excuse to report our day to each other.

Waed decided to stay in Syria and keep her job. Her recent engagement hasn't affected our bond and daily sharing. The difference is the medium, that is, we can only chat online and see our faces through the phone's camera. I miss her a lot and pray for a reunion one day. She is my soul.

When it was time to enroll the university, I told my parents that I wanted to be an officer like my father. Each and every time I saw the girls in police uniform in Syria, my heart skipped a beat! I wanted to become one of them. However, my father discouraged me from entering the police academy and told that women have more difficulties as officers in Arab countries and lead a harder life than men, facing many dangers. I listened to his advice, he must have witnessed many incidents to come to such a conclusion as an officer.

Instead, I studied law and worked for five years (2004–2009) in a private company which specialized at intellectual property protection. The course that I enjoyed the most at university was the criminal law; I scored 99/100 in the final exam. I have been fascinated by the question why certain people commit crimes. After studying and observing many cases, I decided that the family is the most important structure for the children to turn into good individuals and it affects their whole destiny. If the family lacks a clear set of boundaries and moral codes, the child will most probably turn out to be a person with criminal tendencies too.

Leaving Home with My Younger Sister

The office where I began working after graduation was located in a government-controlled district of Aleppo, but still relatively dangerous to commute. In 2016, things became extremely fragile. I was working until 8 p.m. in the evenings and in one of those days, an anti-government group attacked with grenades and small rockets at around 11 p.m. and destroyed our building completely. Finding still-smoking rubbles on the property where my office stood only the day before was a huge shock. We lost electricity and water in the neighborhood as well. This incident accelerated my decision to leave Syria with my younger sister. Taking the decision was not easy by no means, but my parents supported it too. Our absolute submission and trust to Allah gave us the courage for this incredibly dangerous journey. I knew that crossing the borders as two young and single women was not the wisest thing to do but staying in Aleppo after witnessing the demolition of my office was also very tough.

My 20-year-old sister and I left Syria on March 5, 2016. It was the first time that we separated from our parents and Aleppo. It never crossed my mind to leave my family before marriage. As the older sister, I knew I had to be strong and responsible. My sister is clingy by nature and she lacked the experience in life. She depended on me the entire time. Khirbet Al-Jouz was the name of the mountainous area we had to climb up. I fell down many times and had bruises all over. I couldn't move my body for three days after that journey. We were able to cross to the Turkish border at our second attempt.

When we were caught in Turkey, my sister and I were located into a school building in Kilis. We were given blankets but we preferred to use our jackets to cover ourselves instead. We didn't know who used those blankets before us. We shared the space with some Afghan women and I can tell you that they came from a different background. Their eating and cleaning habits differed fundamentally from us. We were relieved to be released from that place and went on to Izmir to take the ferry to the Greek island of Lesbos. We sold some of the gold we had in Syria in order to pay the smuggler and survive abroad in general. In total, we stayed in Turkey for 10 days and arrived safely in Greece on March 16, 2016.

First, we were at an unclean and unsafe transitory camp on Lesbos island called Moria where we suffered for 20 days. One of the interview officers, an Egyptian lady, kept us in mind and came back later to relocate us to Karatepe camp. She was a Godsent being. Due to the risk of sexual assault, we could never leave our container alone in Moria, not even once. For example, we got up for the morning prayer to wash ourselves at the public restrooms while it was still dark so we all moved together as six women who shared the container. Two of them were Palestinian-Syrians, are you familiar with this minority group? They were expelled from their homeland in 1948 and have become a part of our community by now.

Once we arrived in Karatepe, we felt safe. When a woman complained about harassment there, the man was expelled immediately. The camp had many families, its rules were strict and clear. My sister and I shared the container with the same four women from Moria and unlike most residents, we never had arguments neither in Moria nor in Karatepe. People wondered and half-jokingly kept asking how we maintained it so peacefully so I was concerned about the evil eye effect [*Bidaa laughs*].

Overall, God helped us a lot along the way and I remain very grateful. The interview for family reunification was stressful. We were told that only one sister would be sent to Germany since we were both over 18 years old, and the other would receive asylum in Greece. As soon as my sister heard the news, she began to cry so I told her to calm down and pray. I was very relieved that they chose her for Germany and not me. I was mature enough to take care of myself and live alone if I had to, but she was too young and dependent.

After my sister came to terms with the idea that she would have to travel to Germany by herself, we began to look for a place to rent in Athens. We no longer needed to stay in the camp after the paper work was processed for both of us. It was not too difficult to find a house since God has been with us and heard our prayers all along. One of the translators in Karatepe was an Algerian Muslim man who introduced us to a Syrian interpreter in Athens. We stayed in this Syrian man's house for one week, God bless him, it was very generous of him to host six women! In the meantime, he talked to one of his Greek neighbors who had a larger house in another district so she rented it to us. I don't know if it is true but we were told that she preferred us since we were all women with no children, meaning that the flat would be very clean and well-maintained. In December 2016, we moved in and continued our peaceful cohabitation until 16 March 2017.

It turned out that my sister's concerns of traveling alone were in vain. One of our roommates and her daughter had seats on the same flight and they accompanied each other. She safely joined to one of our siblings in Germany. Eventually, my other three roommates also left the house and I was the only one who needed to stay in Greece for an unknown period of time.

Moving Out, Settling In and Fond Memories of Food

I will never forget the first night I spent in the flat once everybody left. The silence in the house was unbearable. Nothing online helped me to ease the lack of my housemates. I went out the next morning, met a few friends, and told them openly that I would probably lose my mind had I stayed another night in that empty house. Fortunately, a Greek friend, Katerina

Efthimiou, who was volunteering for the Red Cross knew the manager of the City Plaza Hotel and told me that she would try to get a room for me. Miraculously, she did and only in one day! There is no explanation for it other than intervention of God in my view since the extent of favoritism was shameless there. The manager shares responsibilities with an Afghan who sends away many people who are not Afghans. He offhandedly would tell you to put your name on the waiting list but you can forget about it afterward. I know from experience because the City Plaza was the first place where we applied for room in Athens before renting a house. But Katerina managed to get me in this time.

Let me tell you more about the City Plaza. It has become very famous not only in Athens but around the world. You can google it and find many articles and news reports about this exemplary squat.[1] I immediately embraced the non-stop action and all the sounds in the hotel. This place saved my mind and money. I was paying rent for the other flat, but believe me, it was the silence that immediately pushed me out of the house. Needless to say, I am also glad to be saving 300 Euro every month since the squats are rent-free. God bless the occupiers and the volunteers of this hotel, whether they believe in Him or not. One thing is for sure, they are being showered by our daily prayers in many languages! I wonder if such squats for refugees exist in Germany or Sweden where the city or the government staff work under much stricter rules and laws. I haven't heard of any so far.

In the City Plaza Hotel, you can hear a mix of Greek, English, Arabic, and Farsi, and we share responsibilities for preparing and serving the food and cleaning after. The cooking is communal but I secretly cook in the room on my small electric stove because I don't like the taste or the quality of the food. The Afghan cuisine has an unbearable spice, I am yet to figure out what it is, but I definitely don't like it.

I miss our kitchen in Aleppo where we all helped my mom to prepare food especially during the religious feasts twice a year. I don't usually have breakfast but there is no way to skip it when you live with the family. I can be done with one croissant when I am alone. The most refreshing thing in the morning for me is to chew the insides of a few cardamom seeds. Your heart will begin to beat faster if you eat more than 2–3 seeds so you need to be careful. You already know that Syrian coffee is mixed with cardamom powder. I love its taste so much that in addition to the coffee, I chew them as people eat sunflower seeds.

My family's typical breakfast in Aleppo consists of zaatar, olive oil, white [feta] cheese, green and black olives, sliced tomatoes, cucumbers, fresh bread, and red pepper paste. Take one slice of bread, spread red pepper paste, sprinkle olive oil, and put a layer of cheese on top, and you have a feast! Our heaviest meal is lunch and we make sure that we include fresh vegetables in it. Our dinners are very light compared to most people that I know of.

I imitate my mother when it comes to creativity under the circumstances. At the refugee camps, everyone gets the same food but my mother combines things in such interesting ways that people come to her and ask the recipe. By cooking or shaking our share, she extracts a new type of cheese, adds some spices to it and before you know, you have a delicious pizza in the middle of the refugee camp life! I also prepared something that became very popular among the residents of our second camp [*Karatepe*] before my sister and I moved to Athens. As long as you can find pepper and tomato paste, *pizza a la camp* is easier and more fun than you can imagine.

God forgive me for saying this but sometimes it becomes boring to eat the same food every day so I needed to be creative to enjoy my meals on Lesbos. I love both cooking and eating! My favorite foods are *shish barak* and *molehiya* [*The writer's note: When I visited Bidaa at her City Plaza Hotel room in January 2018, she prepared a lovely lunch: super fresh tabbouleh, warm and round pitas which she called "Syrian pizza," which was made up of crumbled feta cheese mixed with hot pepper paste and* zaatar. *Our meal was followed by a double–Syrian coffee, which was actually from Syria as she showed me the package. She offered some chocolate-covered cookies and insisted passionately as any Middle Eastern host would do that I should eat more.*]

More About Family and My Ideas on Relationships with the Opposite Sex

Days fly by without noticing. My parents recently left Syria too and now waiting for their paper work be sorted out in Karatepe camp. I am learning Greek, teaching Arabic to the children of expatriates in Athens whose Arabic is not advanced enough, and I am also preparing for an English proficiency exam. If I can score above a certain level, I will be able to attend the English courses offered at the American College of Greece (ACG). The goal of the program is to give opportunities to 100 displaced students to continue their education as a non-degree student, provide them with skills that they can use either in Greece or in other European countries they move to in the future. I am very excited about it.[2]

I first arrived in Athens without a job of course, and I thought I would lose my mind. I was so used to working hard and earning money in Syria. Even in the evenings, after dinner, we never wasted time. My mother had a deal with a man who purchased our handicrafts. I like watching TV, but I am always engaged in something else while listening to it. Making crochets or canvas craft was part of our evenings and brought us extra income. I told you that my mother is the real boss behind our household management and she has done an excellent job. On the first day of the month, we would hand in our salaries to her and she would decide what to do with money. One month, she would purchase gold for one daughter, another month, it would be the other daughter's turn to get a gold coin. If she wanted to purchase some furniture or renovate parts of the house, then the money would be spent from this common income pool that she controlled.

It doesn't matter that our order is perturbed due to the war because my mother provided us the skills to establish a routine wherever we go and stick to it by working hard. She brought this structure and habits of sharing all the good and the bad from her own family. She is my hero and role model so I pray God that I will become like her one day after I get married and raise my own family. Having a strong and supportive family is the most fortunate thing that a human can have.

Although my immediate family presently live in different countries such as Sweden, Germany, and Greece, we are always in touch thanks to the smart phones. We feel and show respect to our father ever since I can remember. Even today, whenever my father arrives home, we get up to greet and kiss him no matter what we are doing or with whom we are chatting. Our respect is not built on fear but love. My parents are open about men-women relations as long as they are conducted legitimately and that we inform them about our male friends. If a young man wants to know me better, he needs to be comfortable with meeting my parents and then continue our friendship. I got engaged three times and my parents supported me when I took the decision to break the engagement.

Well, each one has a story of course. The first engagement was to my cousin who declared his love for me very strongly and sent his parents to our house. I was not in love with him or didn't even really like him to be honest, but he insisted that once we get married, I would begin to love him. The second one lasted for five months. The fact that my fiancée was stingy and acted as such even at the engagement period bothered me so I decided that it would be a major problem in future. Before making the call to his parents, my father gave me one week to think about it. The third one was making me paranoid about myself. He kept checking on me constantly which wasn't a good sign. He clearly had trust issues. When I didn't answer his phone immediately, let's say, I'd get back to him in 15 minutes, he would make it an issue. I decided that it would be unbearable in the long run.

In Athens, I am approached by young men who intend to get closer. They are surprised when I encourage them to meet my parents even over the internet. They tell me that many girls would hide from their parents that they are seeing men. I respond in return that there is something called engagement, which is an informal premarital contract between a man and a woman and their families. It is a time when both sides have long conversations and learn about each other's character and history. If men want to go out with me, they should meet my parents since I never hide anything from them. There is a line in the Quran: "Do they not realize that God knows their secrets and their private discussions? That God knows all that is hidden?" (9:78). My mother also informs me about sex in the context of marriage and Islam. She always told us that instead of hearsay and misleading stuff that we learn from here and there, it is best to ask her directly about sexual matters as an experienced woman.

Although we were supposed to discuss everything between men and women in Sharia Law course at my department, there were times when the professors were shy about detailing some issues or specific cases. After all, it is the Middle East so they chose to leave certain divorce cases up in the air. For example, if the wife pulls herself suddenly during the intercourse without asking her husband, can it be considered a cause for divorce? My mother explained that even when their baby is crying in the middle of the act, the woman should make a comment first before interrupting the sex. Thus, the answer is yes!

I think the most important pillars of a long-lasting marriage is trust, respecting each other, and being honest in everything. I feel quite strong about this combination. Although marriage needs it the most, I think all relationships in life will last longer if there is respect and trust. Some people may say love but I feel that it can be temporary and expressed in words only. For me, love is not what I say but what I do. Love is a special feeling which goes deep in your heart and creates a strong attachment toward the other person. In fact, if a man trusts me entirely and treats me with respect, love will grow on my part. I also think that sharing the same culture and faith is important. Life and relationships are already complicated; thus, I wouldn't want to marry someone from another country.

My Encounters with Non-Muslims and Our Conversations About Islam

I consider myself a devout Muslim, but have not given much consideration about the practices of Islam before we were displaced. Since I got to

Greece, I have been asked many questions about Islam and the need to provide logical and clear responses became important. One of the first examples that comes to my mind is the following: One day, an officer who was processing my paper work in Athens, commented on my headscarf. He began with a compliment: "You've got such a pretty face," before posing the question "why are you covering your hair?" immediately after. I told him that Mother Mary covered her hair as well, asked him whether he would dare to pose her the same question if she appeared in front of us. He wasn't expecting this response. After a few moments of silence, he objected, saying that times are different now. I am sure he will think twice before asking the same question to another Muslim woman.

There are many other issues that I am constantly interrogated about by non–Muslims; abstaining from pork, alcohol, and premarital sex are among the most popular ones so far. My strongest reference person has been Zakir Neik, a Muslim scholar of comparative religions. His talks and lectures can be found on Twitter and YouTube. We are like messengers here in Europe. People hear a lot of bad things about Muslims. I keep telling them "Read, read, read…. Don't remain ignorant." For the ears which are genuinely ready to listen to us, we need to be prepared.

There are many signs of *kıyamat*, the Day of Judgment, that were mentioned in the Quran and I witnessed some of them after I left Syria. When we were staying at the camp in Lesbos, we wanted to go out one night and explore the town. Oh, my God, I couldn't believe what I saw! With our full naivety, as 5–6 Syrian women, we walked into a place which we thought was a restaurant but it turned out to be a gay and lesbian bar or some sort of a meeting place, I haven't figured it out. It didn't take us more than a few minutes to leave the place as fast as we could once we saw the same-sex couples kissing and doing all kind of stuff. Homosexuality is forbidden in the Quran so what we witnessed was unacceptable. Changing one's sex from a man to woman and the other way around is also a *kıyamat* sign. Israel's announcing Jerusalem as their capital is another recent indication.

When I encounter these signs, I think of *sura* Al Ar'af (the Heights) in the Quran. It is named after the heights of the barrier which will divide the virtuous or good people from the damned on the Day of Judgment. Prophets were sent to towns in the past but not all people were aware of these blessings. Line 96 says: "If the people of those towns had believed and been mindful of God, We would have showered them with blessings from the heavens and earth, but they rejected the truth and so We punished them for their misdeeds."[3]

I meet people from all different countries and belief systems. I enjoy their company because I learn a lot from them. I also like having debates and informing them about what I know about Islam. I can give you several examples. There is an old atheist Dutch woman whom I befriended. She kept asking me about the miracles and I told her that God sent many miracles to humans in all religions and the Quran gave examples to the ones performed by Jesus and Moses. Most people I meet here whether they are atheists or Christians, they are unaware of the Quran's content, which is a pity. They have never read it in its entirety, all they know is hearsay and the media quotations of a few lines here and there. Am I not right in repeatedly begging them "read, please read"? I have one Christian friend from Eritrea who agreed with me when I told her about the Bible, the one that was not endorsed by the Nicaea Council in the fourth century. She knew about it which is not very common among the Christians that I know. Thus, she and I had the common practices of not eating pork and not drinking alcohol. We disagreed on the holy trinity since she was raised to believe that Jesus was the son of God, a *shirk* or idolatry from our point of view as Muslims.

In Syria, we had several Christian friends but they never had alcohol in front of us. In Greece, as in other countries of Europe, avoiding places or gatherings where alcohol is consumed is extremely difficult. I drink my tea and ignore the rest, while asking for forgiveness if my being there is not appropriate in the eyes of God. Explaining the ban on drinking in Islam is easy since the negative effects of alcohol on mind and body are very clear. It doesn't take a genius to see why a religion would ask its followers to avoid alcohol or drugs. Islam completes the previous religions so it is a reminder of the old religions' uncorrupted states. Monotheistic religions are like a tall building and Islam is the end floor of this building.

There are several Christian women missionaries who approached us since we got here. Once I couldn't hold my tongue and told one of them that I knew Jesus better than she did. I began to quote lines from the Quran where the son of Mary was mentioned and implied that my knowledge on her prophet is more recent and reliable than the contested man-made versions that she held in her hands.

I believe Zaik Naik who says that the original Bible also banned pork and alcohol, and adds that any woman with a headscarf can be said to follow the path of Mother Mary. Furthermore, when you think about it, most Christians across the world have been following not Jesus' but our Prophet Mohammed's life style because they get married, raise families, and engage in worldly matters as much as the spiritual realm and practices. They don't turn the other cheek when someone treats them unfairly, do they? They go to court and seek for retribution, which is *shariat*.

I experienced discrimination more than once here in dealing with officials but God wants Muslims to stand strong and not despair. Once at the
state hospital, I was treated unfairly but I stood my ground, went up to the
manager, and complained. It is a long story which took me two days, but I
took care of it. The incident demanded a lot of patience, all because of one
woman who clearly didn't like refugees or women with headscarf. The second
time was on my return to Athens after visiting my parents in Mytilene camp.
I am not sure why but the officer, who was checking the ID cards, did not
accept mine. I believe he thought it was fake. He began shouting at me but I
didn't give in and shouted back to him and said: "This is issued by your own
government and if you can't tell this is an authentic document, that is not my
fault. But it's my right to travel anywhere in Greece with this thing," and literally threw the card back to him. Witnessing the scene, another officer came,
checked my ID, told me to continue. However, I still needed an apology for
being yelled at. Only after I received it, I left for Athens. In terms of camp
conditions, some journalists were exposed to my rant when I asked them: "Is
this Europe, is this what you call a democratic country with human rights?
Animals won't live here!" I told them to go ahead and film me. I am not shy
when it comes to exposing the wrongdoings or hypocrisy. I have always been
a strong person especially when I witness injustice, I get even stronger while
demanding justice. It's my nature.

Filling in Some Gaps for My New Friends and Contrasting the Youth

Through this life story sharing, I also want to inform the people in the
West about the Quran. In daily conversations, I refer to *sura* Imran and *sura*
Mary in particular so please include them in my story. Can't you insert the
passages from our Holy Book where Mary and Jesus were mentioned?[4] Well,
let me at least underline then that Muslims are required to accept and believe
in every single word about Mother Mary and Jesus: The miracles that he performed, his talking in cradle, the birth scene under the date tree when God
provided Mary with food and drink, and ordered her to abstain from conversation. Whenever I read this sura, I feel the pain and anger for slanders
against Mother Mary, yet she remained silent. *Sura* Al Tahrim, aya 12th mentions Mary as the daughter of Imran, who "guarded her chastity, so We
breathed into her from Our spirit. She accepted the truth of her Lord's words
and Scriptures: She was truly devout." Mary is the only woman in the Quran
identified by name and a chapter (sura) is named after her. Some scholars

accept her as a Quranic prophet too, and many baby-girls are named after her not only in Syria but also in other Muslim countries in the Middle East. I know several Maryams in Aleppo. This naming can demonstrate our respect, love, and acceptance of Jesus' Mother, don't you think? I wonder if I will ever meet Christian baby-girls in Greece or anywhere in Europe or America named Amina or Khadija?

Some of the non–Muslims I have met are angelic people. They are generous, honest, kind, hardworking, and whatnot. In short, they live like how I believe true Muslims should live and act. I can't help but think "they're missing only *shahada*" so I talk about Islam with them too. In fact, we hear that there are several conversions going on for both sides. Many young people who grew up Muslim are converting to Christianity or denouncing all religions because of the immoral things executed in the name of Islam. However, there are people who are involved in deep research and reading regarding the Quran in its entirety, resisting the current negative images of Islam. These seekers eventually convert and become Muslims. They lead more self-controlled and modest lives after denouncing several so-called freedoms in their countries.

I've got a 22-year-old Spanish friend who is very beautiful both physically and in her heart. However, she keeps dating different men and comes back to me either brokenhearted or simply not satisfied, and next thing you know is that she spends the following night with another guy. I feel sorry for her and she teases me in return for not doing it. I hope to convince her to be more selective and get to know men better in character before she sleeps with them. You know, it is because of this illusion of personal freedom thing in the West. She left her family when she was only 18 and since then, she has been pretty much by herself. There are so many women like her but she is the one whom I became friends with. In Syria, we used to hear about these life styles and watch American movies where young people leave home once they finish high school. Most don't even receive financial support from their parents either by choice or due to their parents' decisions. 18 is too young to begin a life of one's own if you ask me. They are still in need of emotional and other kinds of support that they no longer can get from home. Then, they bear the consequences of filling the gap as in the case of my Spanish friend. She is not happy with all these men she spends time with, they are temporary games or seductions, maybe entertainment. If God forbids premarital and illegitimate sex, it is for one's own benefit, not for God. For me, this is as clear as daylight. What good or harm is it for the almighty Allah that you have sex with a different man every week? I'd bring a similar argument for the iddah period for widows or divorcees mentioned in the Quran. Why is it 4 months and 10 days? There is a reason for everything that God ordered for our own benefit. Some of these things are scientifically but only recently proven and many of them are yet to be.

I know I said this before but the family is the strongest pillar in one's life and will help young people to avoid making many mistakes that they will regret later in life. Some of these mistakes may be hard to mend too such as drug or alcohol addiction.

Joys of Life and Future: Languages, Children and Traveling

My future plans have been changed by the circumstances but I feel fine as I believe in destiny and do my best to adapt and continue to work hard in wherever I am. I hope to be both a teacher and a student of foreign languages. If I could, I would teach the whole world Arabic to make them realize how rich and special my mother tongue is. I love working with children so teaching them languages sounds like an excellent combination to me. Being a student of Greek and in near future of German is also exciting. I am getting more advanced in English, which is the most popular language of our times.

I used to visit my sister's children regularly, and we had so much fun, well, which included a bunch of loud songs and screams, and drove my mother crazy. I wasn't even aware of the noise since I would forget myself in their world and become one of them. In short, I may not practice law in future but instead become an educator and work specifically with children. God will show me the way and I have been curiously watching and contributing to the new life that unfolds in front of me after 2016.

The best birthday gift that I have ever had was my new passport which arrived exactly on February 2, 2018! Now I have the freedom to travel legally around the world. It is called a "Geneva passport" which I received in a bit less than two years since my journey from home began. My first trip will be to Germany in March for ten days to see my sisters, then I will come back to Athens. [*Bidaa shows me her "Document of Freedom" whose light blue cover has the golden words of "Hellenic Republic, Travel Document (Convention of July 28th 1951)"*]

Overall, I like being in Greece because many things in daily life here reminds me of home; the same disorder, the same craziness, the overflowing garbage, the same weather, the same traffic where no rules apply, and loud people. They are friendly and naïve too. I guarantee you that if the Greek government functioned properly as the German government did, no Syrian would want to go to Germany. Based on my Syrian friends' reports, they are more rigid and obsessed with rules and orders, which is not like Syria. Plus, I was told that Germans are suspicious of you and ask many questions. I hear that the weather is depressing too.

Sometimes my Greek friends ask: "How was Syria, Bidaa, how did it look like before the war?" I tell them to take a walk in Monastiraki and they'll know how it is like to wander around Aleppo. They are always surprised by my response for they expect Greece to be very different from Syria but in truth, we're very similar! Whenever I get homesick, I go to Monastiraki.

Another country I'd like to visit is Japan. I admire their culture, technology, and brain power. I read somewhere about the way they discipline their children and it was very similar to our Prophet's sayings. I watch some of their inventions on YouTube and they look like sci-fi movies to me. Japanese people dream the impossible and then make them come true, which should be an example for all of us. We joke that my older sister in Sweden had it the Japanese style! Even as a child, she used to tell us in detail how she'd learn English and then move to Europe one day. See? First dream, even if people think you are crazy, and then they will come true!

After I watch these amazing Japanese machines or inventions for the benefit of humanity online, I think of Syria where brother is killing brother, and for what? For nothing! What a contrast between the two countries! If Syrians were smarter, they wouldn't have fought. Here in Athens, there are Christians and Muslims now all living together but we don't fight or wage war. Hate is dangerous and fatal. Mohammed didn't kill other people for disbelieving or disrespecting him. In Syria, people became very judgmental and began killing each other. It is a shame.

Challenging Closures

An Open-Ended Evaluation

There is a Turkish proverb which captures my long and frustrating process of search for funding and dealing with the paper work throughout the project: "By the time the wise person looks for a bridge, the crazy one has crossed the water."[1] Another way to describe how I work is "daringly," which sometimes borders a line between courage and stupidity, always tinged with uncertainty. The way I define courage is to put one's heart into one's work. In French, the same word originates and means "heart" as well as "innermost feelings." Madeline Gagnon informs her readers that the word "knowledge" and "co-birth" (co-naître, naître avec) are etymologically linked in the word "connaître" which means "to know." Thus, to be born with the other, whether it is a person or an event, would "entail giving birth to a new and different self."[2] Accordingly, to know the other, in this case Syrian refugee women and their lives, meant to be born with them through this narrative inquiry project and inevitably has led to a better knowledge of myself at the end of the journey.

Rose, Lutfia, Muzna, Sama, Emilia, Zizinia, Leila, Sara, Bidaa, and I have trouble with farewells. One succinct way of parting is to make a list of converging and diverging themes that arose from the narratives. The list might help me overcome my farewell anxiety.

1. The Father Figures. Six out of nine women recalled their childhood with fond memories and praised their fathers in particular. These men stood out as more progressive and compassionate toward their daughters than most of the men in their circle. The representations of the Syrian fathers in the book are conspicuously positive and admirable, and they challenge the oppressive Middle Eastern and/or Muslim men stereotype who prioritize their sons over daughters. Four out of nine women chose their fathers as their heroes from an unlimited number of real or fictional, dead or alive figures.

2. The Rich Diversity in Religious Beliefs and Practices. Unfolding of the heterogeneity of Islam, preeminently of the Sunnis in Syria, was not among my aims when I began this project. However, I am glad it surfaced as an outcome. The main concern for any scholar in the representation analysis or imagology studies is to become complicit with the stereotypes that one is critical of. I am no exception. However, after reading this book, I don't think anyone can make sweeping misjudgments about Islam and how it is practiced in contemporary Syrian society. The narratives of Leila and Zizinia notably need further probing since they self-identified as Sunni Muslims and constantly defy the conservative and covered Sunni Muslim female figure.

3. Placing Education Above Everything. The importance of getting a formal education was a collectively agreed and supported asset that each Syrian woman co-participant made sure to acquire at all costs. It was also an intergenerational effort; all parents planned and worked for their children's education. The sacrifices made for a university diploma ranged from a participant's hunger strike to another's commuting to campus under severe bombardment risks. Rose, Lutfia, and Zizinia, the three mothers of the nine women, continuously mentioned concerns about their children's education. Zizinia chose her two daughters as her "heroes" for surviving displacement, learning a new language, and emerging as successful students in their new schooling in Turkey.

4. Homesickness and Adaptation(s). Because of the dramatic changes in climate and food, I wonder how alienated the refugees must feel after their resettlement processes are over. On the surface, they enjoy having access to better technology and democracy in Europe and Canada to begin with, and to be fair, the list of privileges in the host country is a long one. However, most refugees and international students love to complain about the weather and the food, which makes me think that only these two can define home. Whether resettlement is in Germany, Sweden, or Canada, they never feel at home. In the case of Syrians in Turkey, the situation might be different. They may feel more at home because of similar food and climate, but they still lack democracy and the basic rights of a refugee such as effective protection and access to jobs and services. Both participants who sought asylum in Greece expressed pleasant feelings of being at home in Athens due to people's general characteristics, food and climate. In fact, I met Zoe Holman, an Australian writer who made Athens her home last year, who is writing on the real and imaginary borders between Europe and the Middle East as she herself was struck by the cultural resonances in Greece.

5. Appreciation and Healing Aspect of Documenting One's Life Story. Sharing life stories can heal individuals when they feel "broken" and help them move forward to novel understandings of self and their social and spiritual world. I am not a therapist but I know of mental health professionals who employ narrative therapy in their work in order to help their clients to reframe their life stories in a more holistic and integrative way than in the past.[3]

Every co-participant expressed positive feelings regarding their process of narrative inquiry. The year 2011 was the year of crackdowns of many things, and this included their own selves. A confusing identity fragmentation followed when the women's memories kept failing them. Everything was "before" or "after" the revolution or war, so bringing these two parts made the respondents "complete" again as Zizinia put it. Emilia being the exception, none of the women thought their lives worth recording or writing before the project began.

Lego Bricks: Improving Communication, Critical Thinking and Creativity

The work of re-authoring one's identity and life story helped nine displaced women to remember and identify their values, skills, and knowledge that have been disjointed since 2011. It offered them some quality time in a safe space to determine what they might think is possible before them, especially when they responded to the questions on future dreams and possibilities.

Unlike the narrative therapist who reinterprets the clients' episodes as learning experiences and makes suggestions on approaching events and people from different perspectives, I have hardly made comments or developed solutions to the women's problems while listening. It was only after our meetings that I might have modestly offered some help or contacted someone whose connections or resources were of some assistance. However, they were the extensions of organically developed bonds of friendship.

Shifting viewpoints and befriending the reader with nine resilient and smart individuals with promising futures have been my not-so-secret plan. During the process and afterward, I was delighted to be thanked more than once for my skills of listening and writing. I was surprised that the process provided women co-participants a clear sense of self-confidence and agency where the self-reflection was essential. It also proved to be therapeutic. Our friendship, exchange of ideas, and personal news will continue. Our collective hope is to enrich and feminize the discussions on refugees worldwide.

The reader will derive further threads and contribute to the above list so I am comfortable keeping it brief for this volume. I will spare my analysis on the researcher-subject relations in social sciences and oral history here and will publish them elsewhere as I did in the past (Ezer 2017, 57–76; Ezer 2015, 37–47). After years of practice, I came to the conclusion that listening to people is a delicate art form, which requires a certain personality and talent. However, one can achieve an actual success only through crafting and patience. A life story interview is "best carried out as an art," and "just as there are better artists, there are good and better interviewers, the execution of the interview will vary from one interview to another" (Atkinson 2007, 236).

The scientists claim that playing with Lego develops problem-solving and organization while improving communication and critical thinking. It also triggers creativity in children. The resemblance between a colorful set of stackable, interlocking pieces and the moments of life stories is striking to me. Refugee narratives can be assembled and re-assembled in infinite possibilities too, depending on who is playing with them in the adults' world. I am a team player and dedicate my Lego bricks to cultivating communication and creativity among the grownups across the globe. I hope to re-assemble or interlock many more pieces of treasured and dreaded moments in people's lives. I wish they were made up of suger-cane bioplastic, too, but they are not. If only we knew…

Glossary

Alawites: They are a sect of Shia Islam, primarily centered in Syria. They revere Ali, who is considered the first Imam of the Twelver school. The French Mandate of Syria marked a turning point in Alawi history since the French recruited Syrian civilians into their armed forces, creating exclusive areas for minorities, including an Alawite State. Since Hafez al-Assad took power in 1970, the Syrian government has been dominated by a political elite led by the Alawite Al-Assad family.

Amina: Mohammed's mother, who gave birth to him two months after her husband died in 571. She died when he was 6 years old. Mohammed was raised by his grandfather Abd al-Muttalib and later, his uncle Abu Talib.

Amir/emir: Governor of a province; a military commander.

Assyrian: Assyrian people are an ethnic group indigenous to the Middle East. They speak East Aramaic languages and the dominant language in their countries of residence. They are typically Syriac Christians who claim descent from Assyria, one of the oldest civilizations in the world, dating back to 2500 BC in ancient Mesopotamia.

Aya(h): Literarily, a sign or message, evident in God's creation. A verse of the Quran.

ayıp: Shame or inappropriate behavior.

bayram: The generic name for religious or national festivals in Turkey.

fattoush: A type of Middle Eastern salad consisting of croutons (typically of toasted pitta bread) mixed with chopped tomatoes, cucumber, and often other vegetables and herbs.

Gurdwara: (Punjabi: "doorway to the Guru") A place of worship in India and overseas. The *gurdwara* contains a copy of the *Adi Granth* ("First Volume"), the sacred scripture of Sikhism. It also serves as a meeting place for the congregation, weddings, and initiation ceremonies.

Hadith: The body of traditions relating to Muhammad, which now form a supplement to the Qur'an, called the Sunna.

halal: Sanctioned by Islamic law and ritually fit for use.

haram: Anything that is forbidden or proscribed by Islamic law.

harem-selamlık: It is a seating and/or socializing style where men and women interact separately.

Hegira/hejira: (1) Prophet Muhammad was forced to flee his native city, Mecca to Medina in 622, to escape persecution from those who rejected his message. This event marked the beginning of the Islamic era; (2) Any exodus or departure when undertaken to escape from an undesirable situation.

Inshallah: "If Allah wills (it)." It is a very frequent pious phrase among Muslims.

Khadija: Mohammed's first wife, the first Muslim, 15 years older, a business woman who proposed to Mohammed. They were monogamously married for 25 years. Hatice is the Turkish equivalent.

khayr: Benevolent, good, well-being.

kibbeh: A mixture of meat, bulgur or rice, onion, and seasonings, ground together and served in the form of croquettes stuffed with a filling.

labni/labneh: Middle Eastern version of cream cheese, typically rolled into small balls, served with olive oil and used as a condiment.

mawlid: The birthday of a prophet or saint, used especially in reference to that of Muhammad.

molehi(y)a/molokhia: It can be made from fresh, dried or preserved leaves of the molokhia plant; has a slippery consistency like okra. It is cooked mostly with chicken, rabbit, or beef across the Middle East, including Cyprus.

murshid: A Muslim religious teacher, most commonly used in the context of Sufism, where a spiritual guide who initiates a postulant into a mystical order.

narghile: Water-pipe for smoking, hookah.

Newrouz: (also spelled Nowruz) It means "the New Day" It is the day of the vernal equinox, marks the beginning of spring in the Northern Hemisphere, March 21. Lighting fire, dancing around or jumping over it are among the common traditions.

qat/khat: A native shrub of Arabia, where it is extensively cultivated for its leaves, the narcotic drug obtained from the leaves of this plant.

salep/tha'leb: A hot, creamy, mildly sweet, and nutritive drink consumed during winter. It is made from the dried tubers of various orchidaceous plants.

sambusak: Savory Middle Eastern turnover pastry hand-pies stuffed with cheese and fresh herbs.

shahada: Profession of the Islamic faith, in which one testifies that there is no god but God, and Mohammed is His Prophet.

sheikh: Literally "elderly man," the head of a Muslim religious order or community; a religious doctor or preacher.

shish barak: A traditional dish, probably of Ottoman origins (hence the name), which is made of small meat dumplings cooked in a plain yogurt stew.

Sunnis: Sunni Islam is the largest denomination of Islam. Its name refers to the exemplary behavior of Prophet Muhammad. The differences between Sunni and Shia Muslims arose from a disagreement over the choice of Muhammad's successor and acquired broader political, theological, and juridical significances in time.

Sura(h): The term for a chapter of the Quran, each sura is divided into verses. There are 114 surahs in the Quran, the shortest has three, the longest has 286 verses.

tabbouleh: An Arabic vegetable salad made with crushed wheat/bulgur.

WUSC: The World University Service of Canada.

Yazidis: As a historically misunderstood group, the Yazidis are predominantly ethnically Kurdish, and have kept their syncretic religion alive for centuries, despite oppression and threatened extermination. The religion includes elements of ancient Iranian religions as well as elements of Judaism, Nestorian Christianity, and Islam. The Yazidis had been denounced as infidels by Al-Qaida in Iraq, a predecessor of ISIS, which sanctioned their indiscriminate killing. They lived primarily in northern Iraq, southeastern Turkey, northern Syria, the Caucasus region, and parts of Iran. Yazīdī mythology says that they were created separately from the rest of humankind, being descended from Adam but not from Eve. Marriage outside the community is forbidden. (adapted from: https://www.britannica.com/topic/Yazidi, https://www.theguardian.com/world/2014/aug/07/who-yazidi-isis-iraq-religion-ethnicity-mountains)

zaatar: A condiment made from several Mediterranean herbs and spices (especially wild thyme), with dried sumac, toasted sesame seeds, and salt; consumed at breakfast in the Middle East.

Chapter Notes

Chapter 1

1. Şahintepe is one of the squatter settlements known as "gecekondu" although the city is being transformed through government intervention and mass housing projects.

Chapter 2

1. The author's note: I was shocked to hear this, so we repeated the question to confirm Lutfia's response that she wished to be beaten as a child. How mysterious the human mind remains.

2. Lutfia spent many hours detailing these anecdotes which I chose to discard due to three main reasons: They would dominate the narrative; I was sure that the family (herself included) wouldn't feel comfortable with exposing the anecdotes in the long run. Finally, they were very similar in nature and caused a lot of friction among families even before the marriage began.

3. Based on these accounts, Lutfia's family followed a strict version of Islam where the verbal divorce and three-month-long waiting period (*iddah*) was practiced with no grounds other than their interpretation of Sharia law. These practices had no recognition of the secular government of Syria because the Syrian Arab Republic was founded on the principles of Baathism, which promotes secular Arab nationalism, Arab socialism, and militarism.

4. The NGO coordinator wanted the organization and the staff to remain anonymous.

Chapter 4

1. Sama was asked repeatedly for details and she claimed not remembering, which is highly possible. She kindly evaded many questions although they were posed at different times over a period of ten months. As the reader will notice the way she explains the ten-day-long journey is report-like with no mentioning of any sensory detail.

Chapter 6

1. *Mahshi* is squash stuffed with rice and sometimes meat and cooked mostly on the stovetop. The meat version is served hot, as a main course.

2. According to several internet sources and media news, Father Paolo was exiled from Syria by the government in 2012 for meeting with members of the opposition and criticizing the Assad regime. He was kidnapped by ISIS on July 29, 2013. Ironically, his dissertation title was "About Hope in Islam," completed in 1989.

3. Zizinia decided not to wear a headscarf after summer 2017. In January 2018, she began working for RM Team International in order to experience new challenges and to give her colleagues in Space of Hope more responsibilities.

Chapter 7

1. Leila's father arrived in Istanbul on August 13, 2017. He spent some quality time with the family and is back to Bahrein.

2. As of October 2017, Leila wrote me that they broke up.

3. Fethullah Gülen (b. 1941) is a Turkish Muslim cleric, living in self-imposed exile in Pennsylvania since 1999. The Turkish President Erdoğan accuses him of running a "parallel" structure to the Turkish government with the aims of overthrowing the president. He wants the U.S. to extradite him to Turkey. Gülen says Erdoğan staged the attempted coup himself while Erdoğan announced him as a traitor.

Gülen founded several schools and universities across Turkey and abroad.

4. Leila's Turkish is excellent. I was so surprised and caught myself many times thinking "How can she speak so fluently and without an accent?" Some people have special talents.

Chapter 8

1. Sara's only condition before agreeing this interview was to keep the NGO's name anonymous.

Chapter 9

1. Squats are occupied buildings or lands where people reside without permission or paying rent to the owner. Some are owned publicly, some privately. Some serve as housing squats, others function as social centers, with its activities ranging from distribution of clothing and food to the creation of spaces for political organizing and (legal) info-points. Most of these squats can be found in the neighborhood of Exarchia, with its history of autonomous self-organization and a strong anarchist movement in Athens. The City Plaza Hotel shuttered its doors in 2010 in the wake of the European financial crisis. It was built in 2004 for the Olympics, the business subsequently fell into bankruptcy amid allegations that the owner fled without paying the workers' final salaries. But on April 22, 2016, a consortium of Greek anarchists, leftists, and international volunteers calling themselves the Solidarity Initiative for Political and Economic Refugees broke the locks, reconnected the utilities, cleaned up the rooms and occupied the building. Then they opened it up to 400 refugees fleeing wars in the Middle East, Africa, and Afghanistan. City authorities have taken no steps to try to evict the hotel's new residents, perhaps relieved that it means a few hundred less refugees

for them to deal with. [Adapted from http://time.com/4501017/greek-anarchists-are-finding-space-for-refugees-in-abandoned-hotels.]

2. Bidaa qualified for the course and began her classes on 15 January 2018. It takes place weekdays from 10 a.m. until noon.

3. Bidaa's source for the signs of kıyamat remained unclear to me. I asked her several times for clarifications since none of what she told me as signs are stated in the Quran. She said they are generally hinted, and she trusted the interpretations of the Islamic scholars that she followed such as Zaik Naik.

4. I told Bidaa that fulfilling her request would mean to insert 10–12 pages of quotations. I am still not so comfortable for declining her wish because it is her story after all and if getting these words across means a lot to her then I fail here. In order to do justice, I would recommend the interested readers to visit the suras Imran and Meryem from the Quran (Oxford World Classics, trans. Abdel Haleem).

Challenging Closures

1. Akıllı köprü arayıncaya dek, deli suyu geçer. http://tdk.gov.tr/index.php?option=com_atasozleri&arama=kelime&guid=TDK.GTS.59bd61e2d6f5c0.76255821

2. Madeline Gagnon, 2009, "Being a Writer on Women, Violence, and War," in Not Born a Refugee Woman—Contesting Identities, Rethinking Practices (New York: Berghann), 151.

3. Mary Allen, 2012, Narrative Therapy for Women Experiencing Domestic Violence: Supporting Women's Transitions from Abuse to Safety (London: Jessica Kingsley Publishers).

Also, closer to my perspective: Michael Guilfoyle, 2014, The Person in Narrative Therapy: A Post-Structural, Foucauldian Account (Houndmills, Basingstoke: Palgrave Macmillan).

Bibliography

Abul Fadl, Amani. 2005. *Birds of the South.* Beirut: Dar Al-Fikr. "Akıllı köprü arayıncaya dek, deli suyu geçer." http://tdk.gov.tr/index.php?option=com_atasozleri&arama=kelime&guid=TDK.GTS.59bd61e2d6f5c0.76255821

Alexievich, Svetlana. 2016. *Second Time— The Last of the Soviets.* Translated by Bela Shayevich. New York: Random House.

_____. 2017. *The Unwomanly Face of War: An Oral History of Women in World War II.* Translated by Richard Pevear and Larissa Volokhonsky. New York: Random House.

Allen, Mary. 2012. *Narrative Therapy for Women Experiencing Domestic Violence: Supporting Women's Transitions from Abuse to Safety.* London: Jessica Kingsley Publishers.

Atkinson, Robert. 1998. *The Life Story Interview.* Thousand Oaks, CA: Sage.

_____. 2007. "The Life Story Interview as a Bridge in Narrative Inquiry." In *Handbook of Narrative Inquiry Mapping a Methodology,* edited by Jean Clandinin, 167–95. Thousand Oaks, CA: Sage.

Bauer, Wolfgang. 2016. *Crossing the Sea: With Syrians on the Exodus to Europe.* Los Angeles: And Other Stories.

Bordoni, Linda. "Father Paolo Dall'oglio: 'Bridge-Builder' in Syria." Accessed August 29, 2017. http://en.radiovaticana.va/news/2017/07/28/father_paolo_dalloglio_bridge-builder_in_syria/1327542

Cain, Susan. 2012. *Quiet: The Power of Introverts in a World That Can't Stop Talking.* New York: Crown Publishers.

Chaucer, Geoffrey. 1914. *Canterbury Tales.* New York: Duffield. http://www.librarius.com/canttran/manlawtr/manlawtale841-861.htm

Cockburn, Cynthia. 2014. "Exit from War: Syrian Women Learn from the Bosnian Women's Movement." *Interface: A Journal for and About Social Movements* 6(1): 342–62.

Di Giovanni, Janine. 2016. *The Morning They Came for Us—Dispatches from Syria.* New York: Liveright Publishing.

Ezer, Ozlem. 2015. "Women's Life Writings from a 'No Wo/Man's Land': Northern Cyprus." In *Not Ever Absent—Storytelling in Arts, Culture and Identity Formation,* edited by Sjoerd-Jeroen Moenandar and Nicole Miller, 37–47. Oxford: Inter-Disciplinary Press.

_____. 2017. "Oral History Narratives as Becoming: Traces in Northern Cyprus." In *Stories of Becoming—The Use of Storytelling in Education, Counselling and Research,* edited by Sjoerd-Jeroen Moenandar and Lynn Wood, 57–76. Nijmegen: Campus Orleon Publishing.

Gagnon, Madeline. 2008. "Being a Writer on Women, Violence, and War" in *Not Born a Refugee Woman—Contesting Identities, Rethinking Practices,* edited by Maroussia Hajdukowski-Ahmed, Nazilla Khanlou, Helen Moussa, trans. Lori-Ann Moulton. 150–162. New York: Berghahn.

Geiger, Susan. 1990. "What Is So Feminist About Women's Oral History?" *Journal of Women's History* 2.1: 169–182.

Guilfoyle, Michael. 2014. *The Person in Narrative Therapy: A Post-Structural, Foucauldian Account.* Houndmills, Basingstoke: Palgrave Macmillan.

Kabbani, Nizar. 2010. *Republic of Love: Selected Poems in English and Arabic.* Translated by Nayef al-Kalali. Edited by Lisa Kavchak. New York: Routledge.

Madre.org. 2014. "Seeking Accountability and Effective Response for Gender-Based Violence Against Syrian Women: Women's Inclusion in Peace Processes." Accessed August 23, 2017. https://www.madre.org/sites/default/files/PDFs/Women%27s%20Inclusion%20in%20Peace%20Processes.pdf

Matson, William. 2016. *Crazy Horse: The Lakota Warrior's Life & Legacy*. Layton, UT: Gibbs Smith.

Ohchr.org. 2014. "CEDAW 58th Session." Accessed August 8, 2017. http://tbinternet.ohchr.org/_layouts/treatybodyexternal/Download.aspx?symbolno=CEDAW%2fC%2fSYR%2fCO%2f2&Lang=en

Pearlman, Wendy. 2017. *We Crossed a Bridge and It Trembled—Voices from Syria*. New York: Custom House.

The Quran. 2010. Translated by M.A.S. Abdel Haleem. Oxford: Oxford University Press.

Rasamny, Malek, and Matt Peterson. 2017. "The Native and the Refugee." Accessed August 10, 2017. https://thenativeandtherefugee.com/

Shafak, Elif. 2010. *The Forty Rules of Love*. New York: Viking.

Stowe, Harriet Beecher. 1852. *Uncle Tom's Cabin*. Boston: Houghton Mifflin. https://archive.org/details/uncletomscabin00stow

"Who Are the Yazidis and Why Is Isis Hunting Them?" Accessed March 23, 2018. https://www.theguardian.com/world/2014/aug/07/who-yazidi-isis-iraq-religion-ethnicity-mountains.

Wikipedia. n.d. "The Rose of Versailles." Accessed August 4, 2017. https://en.wikipedia.org/wiki/The_Rose_of_Versailles

Wilson, Catherine. 2015. *Epicureanism: A Very Short Introduction*. Oxford: Oxford University Press.

"Womanhood." *OED Online*, Oxford University Press, March 2018, www.oed.com/view/dictionaryentry/Entry/229891. Accessed 10 April 2018.

Yazbek, Samar. 2012. *A Woman in the Crossfire: Diaries of the Syrian Revolution*. London: Haus Publishing.

"Yazidi-Religious Sect." https://www.britannica.com/topic/Yazidi. Accessed 23 March 2018.

Index